THE GATHERING STORM

MILESTONES IN BLACK AMERICAN HISTORY

THE GATHERING STORM

1787 – 1829

From the Framing of the Constitution to Walker's Appeal

Mary Barr Sisson

CHELSEA HOUSE PUBLISHERS
Philadelphia

FRONTISPIECE: An 1852 painting depicting an American slave auction.
ON THE COVER: The anguish of slaves arriving in a strange land.

Chelsea House Publishers
Editorial Director Richard Rennert
Production Manager Pamela Loos
Art Director Sara Davis
Picture Editor Judy Hasday

Milestones in Black American History
Senior Editor Marian W. Taylor
Series Originator and Adviser Benjamin I. Cohen
Series Consultants Clayborne Carson, Darlene Clark Hine

Staff for THE GATHERING STORM
Associate Editor Therese DeAngelis
Editorial Assistant Kristine Brennan
Designer Takeshi Takahashi
Picture Researcher Patricia Burns
Cover Design Alison Burnside
Digital Photo Colorization Robert Gerson

First Printing

1 3 5 7 9 8 6 4 2

Library of Congress Cataloging-in-Publication Data

Sisson, Mary Barr.
The gathering storm: from the framing of the Constitution to Walker's appeal, 1787-1829 / Mary Barr Sisson.

  p. cm. — (Milestones in Black American history)
Includes bibliographical references and index.
Summary: Presents a partial history of slavery and the abolitionist movement in the United States.

ISBN 0-7910-2252-8 0-7910-2678-7 (pbk.)

1. Slavery—United States—History—Juvenile literature. 2. Afro-Americans—History—To 1863—Juvenile literature. [1. Slavery. 2. Afro-Americans—History—To 1863.] I. Title. II. Series.

E446.S613 1996
973.7'114—dc20
                                            95-33528
                                               CIP
                                                AC

CONTENTS

MILESTONES IN BLACK AMERICAN HISTORY

INTRODUCTION

Eleven years after the Declaration of Independence identified the "inalienable rights" of "life, liberty, and the pursuit of happiness," delegates from the former colonies met in Philadelphia to draft a constitution for a new, federal form of government. Tragically, the document they produced left intact the institution of slavery. For the nation's 700,000 African slaves, freedom and equality remained mere words.

In the four decades that followed, slavery grew more entrenched—and more brutal—in the southern states and expanded into the Louisiana Territory. By 1830 the United States had more than two million slaves. Meanwhile, as slavery gradually disappeared in the North, the number of free blacks steadily increased, to nearly 320,000 by 1830.

Yet even free blacks had few rights and faced many restrictions. In Tennessee, for example, free blacks were forbidden from traveling beyond their county of residence. In Virginia a freed slave could be seized and sold back into slavery to settle a former master's debts. Many states restricted blacks from voting, and nowhere could they testify against whites in court.

In the face of this oppression and discrimination, African Americans during the years 1787–1829 followed a variety of paths. Some worked to improve conditions by educating and organizing the black community. In 1787, two former slaves, Richard Allen and Absalom Jones, established the Free African Society, which was dedicated to the advancement of blacks. Allen also founded a society to promote education for black children, and he was instrumental in the establishment of the African Methodist Episcopal church, the first fully independent black church in the United States.

By contrast, other African Americans, such as the merchant and sea captain Paul Cuffe and the editor John Russwurm, doubted that conditions for America's blacks—even free blacks—would ever improve. They turned to Africa as a place where blacks could "rise to be a people." The attempt to settle free blacks in Africa, dubbed the colonization movement, also found support among some proslavery whites, who viewed the presence of free blacks in the United States as a dangerous example for slaves. In 1822, with money appropriated by the U.S. Congress, a group of black colonists settled in Liberia, on the west coast of Africa. Though the Liberian colony grew to more than 1,400 members by 1830, the colonization movement had only marginal impact in America. The majority of African Americans considered the United States their home, and free blacks refused to abandon their enslaved brethren. As an anticolonization statement issued by a free black church stated, "We will never separate ourselves voluntarily from the slave population in this country; . . . we feel that there is more virtue in suffering privations with them, than fancied advantages for a season."

It was this spirit of solidarity that led free blacks to join white abolitionists in organizing the Underground Railroad. By 1808, the Railroad, a series of safe houses through which runaway slaves could pass on their way to the northern United States or Canada, was well established. Eventually it would conduct 100,000 or more slaves to freedom.

For many slaves, however, rising up violently against their masters seemed the only road to freedom. The first three decades of the 19th century saw numerous slave uprisings, large and small. In one such incident in the summer of 1800, about 1,000 slaves in Virginia planned to seize the state capital of Richmond. At the conspirators' trial, one of the men, perhaps the leader of the uprising, 24-year-old Gabriel Prosser, declared, "I have nothing more to offer than what General Washington would have had to offer, had he been taken by the British and put to trial by them. I have adventured my life in endeavoring to obtain the liberty of my countrymen, and am a willing sacrifice to their cause. . . ."

The cause was also adopted by black writers and thinkers, who assailed the evils of slavery directly and, through their talent and learning, undermined its ideological foundations. In a letter he wrote to Thomas Jefferson in 1791, the African-American astronomer and mathematician Benjamin Banneker urged that Jefferson and fellow whites "wean yourselves from those narrow prejudices which you have imbibed . . . and thus shall you need neither the direction of myself or others in what manner to proceed herein."

Less than 40 years later, such a gentle appeal to the conscience of proslavery whites would seem quaint. Slavery had not gradually disappeared, as some abolitionists had naively hoped. Rather, the divisions between black and white, North and South, abolitionist and slaveholder had grown deeper and more bitter. When David Walker published his

Appeal in 1829, he not only urged slaves to kill their masters but also had this dire warning for the entire nation: "I tell you Americans! that unless you speedily alter your course, *you* and your *Country are gone!!!!!!*"

Three decades later, at Bull Run and Antietam, at Fredericksburg and Gettysburg, the consequences of not altering that course would become horribly evident.

MILESTONES
1787–1829

1787
- African-American clergymen Richard Allen and Absalom Jones found the Free African Society in Philadelphia to offer support services to the free black community.

- From May to September, the Constitutional Convention convenes to create the Constitution, the foundation of American government. Debates over slavery threaten to unravel the fragile union, but abolitionist northerners grant several concessions—including a 21-year moratorium on abolishing the slave trade—to appease proslavery southerners.

- A ship carrying some 350 black and 100 white settlers from Great Britain lands at Sierra Leone, Africa; disease and attacks by local Africans decimate the new colony.

1788
- A petition from the African Lodge of the Fraternal Order of the Free and Accepted Masons, led by former slave Prince Hall, results in a law prohibiting the importation, transportation, purchase, or sale of Africans in Massachusetts.

1790
- The census reveals that New Jersey and Pennsylvania each hold more slaves than Tennessee; the North, however, has an equal number of free and enslaved blacks (the northern states depend less on slave labor and are thus more open to manumission).

- In the French Caribbean colony of Saint-Domingue, free mulatto Vincent Ogé dies after leading a black revolt against the colonial government.

- The U.S. Congress prohibits blacks from serving in the armed forces, and many state militias exclude them as well.

1791
- In Saint-Domingue, slaves from more than 1,000 plantations join in a mass uprising; French and Spanish forces both attempt to gain control of the colony.

- *The Interesting Narrative of the Life of Olaudah Equiano, or Gustavas Vassa, the African, Written by Himself*, a memoir describing the horrors of the slave trade and slavery, is published in New York.

1792
- Benjamin Banneker, a free black Marylander, helps survey the site of the nation's future capital; he also publishes the first of a series of popular almanacs.

1793
- The invention of the cotton gin spurs the growth of slave-worked cotton plantations in Mississippi and Alabama. As slavery becomes ever more vital to the ruling class, the South enacts new laws regulating slaves and abolitionists.

1794
- In Saint-Domingue, black rebel leader Toussaint-Louverture helps the French, who had liberated the slaves in their colonies, defeat the Spanish.

- For the first time, the North's many abolitionist societies join in a national meeting.

- Along with pastor Absalom Jones, the Free African Society establishes the St. Thomas African Episcopal Church of Philadelphia; Richard Allen founds the black Methodist Bethel Church.

1798
- The U.S. secretary of the navy allows blacks to enlist.

1800
- Inspired by events in Saint-Domingue, Virginia slave Gabriel Prosser plots an armed uprising against the state capital. Slave informers reveal his plan, and he and 34 of his coconspirators are hanged.

- Prince Hall founds Boston's first black school.

1802
- The forces of French emperor Napoléon invade Saint-Domingue and arrest Toussaint-Louverture, who later dies in prison. Former slave Jean-Jacques Dessalines then leads the island's blacks in expelling the French. In 1804, the victorious blacks will form their own independent republic, Haiti. The United States will refuse to recognize the new nation.

- Connecticut gives free blacks the vote. Other northern states follow suit, but only if the blacks meet stringent requirements such as property ownership. In 1814, Connecticut will withdraw blacks' right to vote.

1806
- Louisiana enacts harsh new slave codes; free blacks throughout the South are also subjected to restrictive laws.

1807
- Congress bans the importation of slaves into the United States.
- Great Britain outlaws the slave trade; when the British Royal Navy intercepts slave ships, it often releases the freed Africans in Sierra Leone.

1811
- Black Massachusetts shipping company magnate Paul Cuffe visits Sierra Leone and receives a special license to trade between the African colony and England, but the War of 1812 between England and the United States delays his plans.

1814
- Future president Andrew Jackson, desperately needing men to help fight the British in New Orleans, recruits two regiments of free black soldiers and promises them the same amount of land as white soldiers receive. The black veterans do not receive their payment until 1823, but their stellar performance prompts other states to recruit black soldiers.

1816
- The U.S. Army destroys a Florida fort defended by runaway slaves. Some 300 women and children are killed in the attack, which triggers the First Seminole War; the Seminole Indians and their black allies fend off the Americans until 1819.
- Cuffe arrives in Sierra Leone with 38 black Americans, who receive a plot of land to farm. Almost bankrupted by huge British cargo taxes, Cuffe leaves Africa for good, although he continues to endorse colonization until his death a year later.
- The American Colonization Society, an organization dedicated to settling free blacks in Africa, is launched in Washington, D.C.; the African-American community opposes the society, fearing that it will force the exodus of blacks who had lived in America for generations.
- Richard Allen is appointed head of the newly established African Methodist Episcopal (AME) church, America's first fully independent black religious organization.

1820
- Congress passes the Missouri Compromise, which admits Missouri as a slave state and Maine as a free state and abolishes slavery in the northern part of the Louisiana Territory.

1821
- Congress admits Missouri into the Union despite a disputed clause in the state's constitution that bars free blacks from entering the state. As slavery continues to spread, abolitionists become more militant.

1822
- Former slave and AME minister Denmark Vesey organizes 9,000 slaves in a plot to take over Charleston, South Carolina; after a house slave betrays the rebels, the authorities execute Vesey and 40 of his coconspirators and strengthen the black codes.

- To hinder blacks from spreading rebellion, the South Carolina legislature requires that all black sailors be jailed as long as their ships are in Charleston harbor; state authorities enforce the law in disregard of international treaties and threaten to secede from the Union if opposed by the federal government.

- With funds from the U.S. Congress, the American Colonization Society sends a group of African Americans to Liberia, an African colony south of Sierra Leone.

1823
- Alexander Lucius Twilight becomes the first known African American to graduate from an American college, receiving his bachelor's degree from Middlebury College; he is followed in 1826 by Amherst College graduate Edward Jones and Bowdoin College graduate John Russwurm.

1825
- A Christmas Eve fire destroys $80,000 worth of Charleston property; acts of arson attributed to slaves continue almost nightly for the next six months.

1827
- The North Carolina state supreme court rules that Quakers cannot purchase slaves because they do not honor the conventions of slavery, buying slaves to make them virtually free and treating them as human beings.

- Russwurm and Samuel Cornish launch *Freedom's Journal*, the nation's first black abolitionist paper.

1829
- When Cincinnati, Ohio, enforces an 1804 statute requiring free blacks to post a $500 bond before settling in the city, more than 1,100 blacks emigrate to Canada.

- Russwurm resigns from *Freedom's Journal* and emigrates to Liberia; he eventually becomes governor of a nearby colony founded by the more liberal Maryland Society.

- David Walker, a former contributor to *Freedom's Journal*, publishes a passionate antislavery manifesto. *Walker's Appeal*, which sanctions violent revolt, generates a fierce outcry from both slave owners and white abolitionists.

THE GATHERING STORM

1

CONVENTIONS

It was the summer of 1787. The revolutionary war had ended four years earlier, and America was set-tling into its hard-won peace. In the newly indepen-dent nation's cities—Philadelphia, New York, Boston, Charleston, and other urban centers—car-penters sawed and hammered, buildings rose, shops and businesses opened, ships crowded the riverfront wharves.

In the sweltering heat of Philadelphia, 55 visitors, representatives of 12 of the former 13 colonies—now called states—had gathered for a revolutionary pur-pose: to reshape the government of the United States of America. (Only Rhode Island was unrepresented, since it had declined to send a delegate.) The first constitution of the new country, called the Articles of Confederation, had been ratified in 1781. Although it was a step toward national unity, it had proved unworkable because the central, or federal, govern-ment was subordinate to that of individual states. Dissension and discontent had been rising, leading to sporadic violence. The convention delegates of 1787

Slaves jump overboard to escape the horrors of a slave ship. Nearly a third of those captured and taken from Africa during the colonial period died before reaching America. The United States Congress banned slave importation in 1807.

hoped to create a new and stronger system that would last for centuries, holding the country together through any crisis. From May 25 to mid-September the delegates debated, argued, and finally compromised, and by September 17 they had hammered out a document they called the Constitution, the foundation on which the United States of America would be built.

To those who opposed slavery, this re-creation of the government seemed promising. In 1787 the nation was home to more than 700,000 enslaved blacks, but the recent victory over England had planted the ideals of equality and freedom deep in American soil. Abolitionism, the crusade to abolish, or end, slavery, was fast gaining ground in the North. Five northern states and the territory that would become the state of Vermont had already freed their slaves, and most states had banned the importation of new slaves. Although the ban actually reflected anti-British sentiment more than antislavery feelings (British traders had been responsible for most slave importations), it did limit the spread of slavery into new areas.

Several important delegates at the convention were noted abolitionists. Other prominent delegates—future president George Washington, for example—owned slaves themselves, but were strongly committed to justice and liberty. The abolitionists hoped that these beliefs would translate into official opposition to slavery, and some of the decisions of the Continental Congress (predecessor of today's U.S. Congress) heightened their optimism.

One such act was the establishment of the Northwest Territory, a vast area including all or parts of modern-day Ohio, Indiana, Michigan, Illinois, Wisconsin, and eastern Minnesota. Parts of this territory had been the property of individual states—Virginia, Massachusetts, New York, and Connecticut—

and the Continental Congress ceded, or granted, the entire region to the U.S. government. Among the new laws governing the territory was one written by Thomas Jefferson, slave owner and author of the Declaration of Independence; this law barred forever the introduction of slavery into the Northwest Territory.

When it came to lobbying (exerting influence on) the delegates of the Constitutional Convention, however, antislavery forces were surprisingly slow and ineffective. Delegate and future chief justice John Jay, for example, was president of the New York Manumission Society (manumission is the act of freeing from slavery), but he failed to present even a statement of the society's position to the convention.

Although the framers of the U.S. Constitution, including George Washington, were strongly committed to justice and liberty, many were slave owners themselves. After intense debate, the delegates to the Constitutional Convention agreed that each slave would count as three-fifths of one person in state population counts and would be considered property in tax assessments.

Another convention delegate, patriot Benjamin Franklin, was president of the Pennsylvania Abolition Society; the Pennsylvania society asked Franklin to present a paper demanding a stop to the importation of new slaves into the country. Franklin refused, fearful that the paper would alienate convention delegates from the southern states.

Franklin's cautious attitude was all too typical of the time. Most white abolitionists in the 1780s were far removed from the fiery advocates of later decades. (Aside from continual acts of slave rebellion, blacks were mostly silent on the issue; denied access to most public forums, they had little choice.) Slavery, most 18th-century abolitionists believed, should be ended gradually—some northern states, for example, had already freed slaves born after a certain date. Many also asserted that former slave owners should be paid for their lost "property," and that freed slaves should be settled elsewhere—in Africa, for example, or west to the frontier—in order to keep the United States as white as possible. Above all, the abolitionists believed that the end of slavery should not result in disorder. Freedom and liberty for blacks was considered secondary to preserving the unity of the new country.

The Constitution reflects this timidity: the words *slavery, slave, black, Negro,* or *African* never appear in the document. Instead the Constitution uses such phrases as "Person held to Service or Labour," "all other Persons" (that is, other than free), and "such Persons as any of the States now existing shall think proper to admit" (a euphemistic way of referring to slaves imported from other countries). These vague terms were employed to prevent implying constitutional approval or disapproval of slavery.

But the issue was constantly on the tongues of the delegates and often arose during discussions of seemingly unrelated subjects. For example, although the

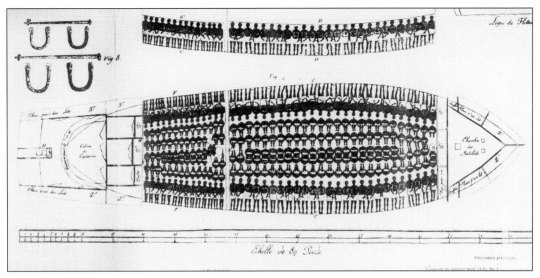

delegates generally acknowledged that slaves would be denied the right to vote, they disagreed on exactly how to account for slaves when determining a state's population. This was not an idle question: though the details had not been resolved completely, it seemed fairly certain that population figures would be used to determine how many representatives—and thus how much political clout—each state would have in the new federal government.

Delegates from southern states, which held the lion's share of the nation's slaves, realized that their region's power in the new government would vastly increase if slaves were included in population counts. Northern delegates, however, had no desire to see a powerful national government dominated by any region other than their own. These men asserted that if slaves were indeed property, then they should no more count as part of the population than barns, cows, or horses. Eventually, the two factions struck a compromise: in determining the number of representatives each state would be allowed, a slave would count as three-fifths of a person; in assessing taxes, each slave would also be counted as property.

A diagram of a French slave ship, showing the placement of "cargo," or slaves, with an illustration of arm and leg shackles (upper left).

Absalom Jones, a former slave, joined the Reverend Richard Allen in 1787 to found the Free African Society. In 1794 Jones assumed the ministry of St. Thomas African Episcopal Church of Philadelphia, the first black-affiliated church in the country.

Although the "three-fifths compromise" excited little outcry among antislavery advocates, it increased the power of the proslavery South in Congress. Most southern congressmen were either wealthy whites who owned slaves or men who owed their positions to those who did, and they were thus united in their support of slavery. Nor did the additional representatives assigned to these states as a result of the three-fifths compromise attempt to represent the interests of slaves. The proslavery block dominated Congress, frustrating federal attempts to regulate slavery and promoting its spread to new areas of the nation.

The slavery issue also complicated the question of trade. With little debate, the delegates decided that the new Constitution would grant Congress the right

to tax and control foreign and domestic commerce.
But when the convention's Committee of Detail rec-
ommended barring Congress from taxing state export
and import of slaves, the delegates exploded. They
viewed the international slave trade as an inhumane
and brutal form of commerce (which indeed it was:
about 30 percent of the slaves taken from Africa died
before reaching the Americas). Even some advocates
of slavery opposed the trade. But the delegates from
Georgia and South Carolina, where slave importation was legal and where slavery was rapidly gaining
ground, insisted on allowing the trade, claiming that
their states' economies would be devastated by
restrictions. The heated debate over slave importation threatened to disrupt the convention. Finally,
Connecticut delegate Roger Sherman suggested that,
in order to keep the convention from disintegrating,
the delegates suppress their opposition to the slave
trade and support the proposal of the Committee of
Detail. Hoping to soothe his fellow northerners,
Sherman maintained that he personally opposed the
slave trade; but why quarrel with the proposal, he
asked, when "the abolition of slavery seem[ed] to be
proceeding throughout the United States"?

Sherman's naively optimistic statement may have
surprised some delegates, but the reply by Virginia
delegate George Mason no doubt surprised many
more. Arguing forcibly for the outlawing of slave
importation, the wealthy and aristocratic Mason
blasted the assembly, claiming that God would
destroy the United States should it fail to end what
he termed the "national sin" of slavery. "Every master of slaves," he thundered, "is born a petty tyrant."
He went on:

> They bring the judgment of heaven upon a country.
> As nations cannot be rewarded or punished in the next
> world they must be in this. By an inevitable chain of
> causes and effects providence punishes national sins by

national calamities. [I hold it] essential to every point of view that the General Government have power to prevent the increase of slavery.

Mason's views were far from common among the delegates, most of whom favored a compromise on the issue. A delegate from the northern slave state of New Jersey proposed that Congress be prohibited from barring the import of new slaves until 1800; southern delegates countered with the year 1808. Despite Virginia delegate James Madison's claim that another 21 years of slave importation would be "dishonorable to the American character," the convention accepted that time period. Considering national unity more important that the abolition of slavery, a number of northern delegates supported the 21-year plan. On the other hand, the delegation from the southern slave state of Virginia (led by Mason and Madison) opposed it. To prevent antislavery forces from taxing the foreign slave trade out of existence, the convention limited to $10 per year per person the taxes the new Congress could place on slave imports.

On August 28, less than three weeks before the convention ended, southern delegates introduced another proposal concerning slavery, which provided for the return of runaway slaves to their masters. Unlike the importation proposal, this one caused almost no controversy, even among the more adamantly antislavery New England delegates.

Throughout the 1780s, provisions for the return of fugitive slaves had been included in treaties between the United States and various Native American tribes. Even the progressive Northwest Ordinance, which established the Northwest Territory and forbade slave trade there, contained such a provision:

No Person held to Service or Labour in one State, under the Laws thereof, escaping into another, shall, in

Consequence of any Law or Regulation therein, be dis-
charged from such Service or Labour, but shall be
delivered up on Claim of the Party to whom such Service or Labour may be due.

The fugitive-slave provision would profoundly
affect the young nation's future. Along with the
three-fifths compromise, it would allow the southern-
dominated Congress of 1850 to pass the Fugitive
Slave Law, a notorious piece of legislation imposing
stiff penalties on those who aided runaway slaves.
The 1850 law would generate massive hostility
between the slaveholding South and the free North,
making the nation's bloody Civil War (1861–65)
inevitable.

When the convention delegates left Philadelphia
in September of 1787, many must have felt proud.
They had forged a new kind of government, strong
and centralized, yet radically different from the old
monarchies of Europe. Though abolition-minded
delegates may have felt uneasy about concessions
made to slaveholders, they could take some comfort
in knowing that the new Constitution did not explicitly condone slavery. Other delegates—Benjamin
Franklin, for example—simply believed that they had
been forced to compromise on some issues. In his
speech on the final day of the convention, the elderly statesman said, "I consent . . . to this Constitution,
because I expect no better, and because I am not sure
that it is not the best. The opinions I have had of its
errors I sacrifice to the public good."

Proslavery delegates, meanwhile, had discovered
that when their opponents faced a choice between
protecting national unity or abolishing slavery, they
seemed willing to make concession after concession.
After all, despite its vague wording, the new Constitution did appear to endorse slavery: it granted
proslavery forces greater congressional power,
restricted the federal government's ability to regulate

slavery, and mandated that all states—free as well as slave" enforce slavery by returning fugitives to their owners.

The nation envisioned by the framers of the Constitution, then, had a place for slavery. But another group of Philadelphia conventioneers had a different vision. A few months before the Constitutional Convention took place, two black Philadelphia clergymen, Richard Allen and Absalom Jones, had founded the Free African Society. The African-American cooperative group's articles of association declared that "a society [of free Africans] should be formed, without regard to religious tenets, provided . . . the persons lived an orderly and sober life, in order to support one another in sickness, and for the benefit of their widows and fatherless children." Although the concept seems far from revolutionary today, the Free African Society was the first organization of its kind—and its founders knew it. Allen and Jones ultimately would dedicate their lives to organizing the black community, first on a local, then on a national, level.

Most white abolitionists seemed willing to entrust progress to mainstream politicians. Black Americans, however, both free and enslaved, were well aware that the American ideals of justice and liberty were not being upheld: slaves had virtually no rights, and the rights of free blacks were sharply limited. Few whites could even imagine a society based on racial equality, but Africans had landed on America's shores before the Pilgrims, and by 1787 blacks had been in America for nearly two centuries.

By the time of the Constitutional Convention, the vast majority of the nation's blacks were second- or third-generation Americans. Born and raised in America, they were far more able to take advantage of existing opportunities than their grandparents had been. The late 18th and early 19th centuries would witness an explosion of black organizations, from the eminently respectable Free African Society to secret associations of slaves plotting violent large-scale uprisings. At the same time, the institution of slavery would grow in power and cruelty until it nearly tore the new country apart.

2

THE CHANGING FACE OF SLAVERY

Despite weakness on a national level, the anti-slavery movement showed surprising strength in individual states in the North. Contrary to many of today's assumptions, slavery was not an exclusively southern practice in colonial America. While upper New England had very few slaves—the 1790 census revealed none in Massachusetts, for instance—other "Yankee" states had many. New York State, for example, boasted a higher slave population in 1790 than did Kentucky, and Pennsylvania and New Jersey each held more slaves than did Tennessee. Still, slavery as an institution was less important to the North's economy, in part because of the increasing number of European immigrant laborers, who generally entered the country through northern seaports. African Americans made up 14 percent of New York's population in 1756; 15 years later that number had declined to 12 percent, and by 1790 it was only 6 percent.

A Georgia cotton field harvested by slaves. Cotton flourished in the climate and soil of the American South. Because it was easier to harvest and required fewer laborers than sugar and rice, early abolitionists believed that cotton's growing popularity would improve slaves' working conditions.

In 1790 the number of free blacks living in the North was nearly two-thirds the number of enslaved blacks in the area: the year's census for the northern states lists 31,008 free blacks and 49,257 slaves. Even in the mid-Atlantic states, nearly one-third of approximately 50,000 blacks were free. In contrast, the South's 657,527 slaves vastly outnumbered their 32,357 free counterparts. This vast difference in the proportion of free blacks to slaves was due at least in part to the North's numerous local and state abolition societies, which held their first national meeting in 1794. Because the North already had a significant free black population, northern whites were considerably less fearful of the potential social effects of abolishing slavery than were southerners.

The ideals of liberty and justice that sparked the American Revolution also inspired many northern states to provide for the gradual emancipation of slaves before the 1787 Constitutional Convention. Even states such as New York, which did not pass comprehensive manumission legislation until 1799, and New Jersey, which did not pass such laws until 1804, had long made it easier for owners to free their slaves. (New York had passed a manumission law as early as 1785, but the state's Council of Revision vetoed it because it denied African Americans the right to vote.) These states had also provided freedom for slaves under special circumstances—for example, if the slave had served in the American military during wartime. In many states, the law allowed owners to free slaves born after a certain date (usually at some point after the passage of the legislation). In other cases slaves remained in bondage until they reached a certain age, and northern slave owners could turn a quick—and legal—profit by selling slaves south before they reached the age of manumission.

Consequently, legal release could be painfully slow in coming. In New Jersey, for example, the abolition process was so gradual that a handful of slaves witnessed the 1860 election of President Abraham Lincoln. The object of such inch-by-inch abolition was to make it easier not for slaves to adjust to freedom but for their owners to avoid financial hardship. Few abolition laws compensated slaves for their years of unpaid labor. Some states, such as New York and New Jersey, were so reluctant to offend slave owners that they offered to reimburse owners for raising freed children of slaves.

However faulty, manumission laws greatly restricted slavery and effectively ended the importation of new slaves in the North. At the same time, however, slavery was rapidly expanding in the South. Thus, although the North's slave population was shrinking, the slave population of the United States as a whole was rising from approximately 710,000 in 1790 to 2,238,000 in 1830. And as the demand for slave labor rose, slave prices increased as well: a slave who would have sold for $300 in 1790 brought about $1,000 in 1830.

The expansion of slavery was largely due to one invention: the cotton gin. A plant whose fibrous boll is used to make cloth, cotton flourished in the climate of the American South. In preparation for market, the plant would be stripped of its seeds, a tedious and extremely time-consuming process. In 1793, Eli Whitney, a schoolteacher from Massachusetts, was visiting a Georgia plantation when he learned about the difficulties of processing cotton. Intrigued, he designed a machine with metal teeth for separating cotton seeds from fibers; six months later he produced a working model of the "gin" (short for engine), thereby revolutionizing not only the cotton industry but the whole South.

The technology Whitney applied to his invention was simple and easily copied, and the machine was soon in use throughout the South. A medium-

Eli Whitney's cotton gin, invented in 1793, revolutionized not only the cotton industry but the entire economy of the South. As cotton production expanded into new territories—present-day Louisiana, Alabama, and Mississippi—wealthy plantation owners acquired more slaves, and the South grew more dependent on the slave trade.

size cotton gin required only one or two operators and could separate fiber from seeds more quickly than 50 people working by hand. Because more cotton could be processed with fewer workers, cotton production quickly increased.

To antislavery observers of this period, the growing popularity of cotton as a cash crop at first seemed reason for hope, not alarm. Cotton was easy to grow, an important consideration for those concerned about slaves' working conditions. More important, slave labor seemed less essential to cotton production than to that of sugar and rice, two other popular southern cash crops, and cotton harvesting was not as backbreaking or dangerous. Even small farmers owning few or no slaves began to concentrate on growing the fluffy white bolls.

As the 19th century progressed, however, big plantations with large numbers of slaves produced more and more of the nation's cotton. The plowing and planting methods for cotton crops caused rapid soil erosion and eventually exhausted the rich farmland in Virginia, the Carolinas, and Georgia. In their search for new land, enterprising cotton planters settled in the relatively unpopulated "southwest," or what is now Louisiana, Alabama, and Mississippi. Here authorities granted large, fertile tracts of land to men who already had substantial wealth in cash or slaves. Should such planters receive land that was less than optimal, they had the labor and funds to improve it; a sizable plantation, once established, could produce cotton much more cheaply than could a small farm. Because of their wealth, and because of an often too-familiar relationship with the government land-grant offices, owners of large slave-worked plantations "squeezed out" small farms, and the Deep South's new cotton "kingdom" became a stronghold of slavery. By 1830 the area's big planters owned more than 600,000 slaves—almost as many as had lived in the entire American South in 1790.

As huge plantations advanced south and west and slave ownership increased, southern states grew more deeply committed to slavery. All slave states restricted the activities of slaves, and by the 1820s they had begun to restrict the activities of free blacks and of whites sympathetic to slaves. These states began passing laws making it difficult or impossible for an owner to free a slave without official approval from the state legislature. Some states prohibited members of antislavery societies from purchasing slaves (whom they would presumably set free) and from sitting on juries (which might decide cases concerning the legality of slavery).

Slavery especially influenced political life in South Carolina. The only state to openly import African slaves in the 19th century, South Carolina was noted both for its reliance on slave labor—especially in its coastal rice plantations—and for its fervent defense of slavery. One means of defense was silence: by the 1820s, newspapers in Charleston, South Carolina's capital, had ceased to print any serious debate about slavery and, fearing further black defiance, no longer reported slave uprisings or conspiracies.

But other states were not as committed to maintaining slavery. The relative indifference of their neighbors greatly troubled many wealthy and prominent South Carolinian slave owners, especially in the face of the minor and large-scale rebellions that plagued them. South Carolinians were also disturbed by the thought that the federal government might presume to abolish or to regulate slavery, and a number of rabidly proslavery politicians of the 1820s fueled their fears, causing alarm over even the occasional debates on the subject in Congress. "The only safety of the southern states," South Carolina senator Robert Y. Haynes claimed in 1827, "is to be found in

Fray 17th November 1807

I. Hugh Teebles of Fray in the County of Runfs...
do Certify that I am Entitled to the service of a Negro
Child a Male born of a slave since the Eighth
day of February one thousand Eight hundred
& Seven that the said Child is of the age of
Nine Months & nine days a Called by the name
of Peter. Witness my hand this day & date
above written —

An 1807 document certifying a slaveholder's ownership rights to a nine-month-old child. Since the child of a female slave became the property of her owner, slaves were often encouraged or pressured to bear children.

the want of power on the part of the Federal Government to touch the subject [of slavery] at all."

South Carolina's disdain for federal authority was not limited to speeches. In 1822 the state legislature enacted a law requiring black sailors entering the port of Charleston to be jailed while their ships were docked in order to keep them from fraternizing with and possibly spreading rebellion among the city's slaves. The law violated a U.S.-British treaty giving citizens of the two nations free access to each other's ports; it created an international incident when Charleston officials jailed a free black sailor from the British colony of Jamaica.

Despite repeated protests by both the U.S. attorney general and the British government, South Carolina officials continued to imprison all black sailors entering Charleston. When in 1824 Secretary of State John Quincy Adams sent a message to the governor of South Carolina demanding an end to the arrests, the state senate sent back a defiant reply: "The duty of the state to guard against insubordination or insurrection . . . is paramount [superior] to all laws, all treaties, all constitutions. It arises from the supreme and permanent law of . . . self-preservation; and will never, by this state, be renounced, compromised, [or] controlled . . . with any power whatever."

South Carolina's continued resistance to federal law was accompanied by impassioned rhetoric, echoed in the state's newspaper and political rallies, about seceding (or withdrawing) from the United States altogether. In 1828, during a debate in the U.S. House of Representatives, Congressman William Drayton boldly stated that if South Carolinians held their "slaves at the mercy of the [federal] Government," the state would have little choice but to reconsider staying in the Union. In another debate that year Senator Haynes announced, "Let me solemnly declare, once for all, that the southern States never will permit, and never can permit, any interference, whatever, in their domestic concerns [i.e., slavery], and that the very day on which the unhallowed attempt shall be made by the authorities of the Federal Government, we will consider ourselves as driven from the Union."

Haynes's claim that all southern states were willing to secede was an exaggeration in 1828, and South Carolina itself would not act on his threat for another 32 years. But the spread of slavery throughout the South ensured that more white southerners would find common ground with radicals such as Haynes. Slavery not only ravaged the lives of millions of African Americans, it threatened the political welfare of the country itself.

3

CONDITIONS

As slavery spread through America, the enslaved population more than tripled, exceeding two million by 1830. The lives of these slaves were by no means uniform, of course, but they were identical in one respect: all were legally considered property, not people, and could be bought, sold, seized as payment on debts, and treated as though they were livestock, furniture, or any other form of personal property. As property, they lacked the rights and liberties the government guaranteed all citizens.

The legal fiction that slaves were property could not erase their humanity, however. Unlike horses or tables, they hoped, dreamed, fell in love, escaped, plotted, and defied their masters. In an effort to control the lives of slaves—and to protect their owners—many states enacted special laws called "black codes" or "slave codes." The 1806 Louisiana slave codes read in part, "The condition of a slave being merely a passive one, his subordination to his master and to all who represent him is not susceptible to any modifica-

Slaves labor on a sugar cane plantation. It was not unusual for slaves to work 18 to 20 hours a day during harvest season, and they were routinely beaten for working too slowly or trying to rest.

tion or restriction. . . . He owes his master and family a respect without bounds, and absolute obedience, and is to execute all orders." The Louisiana codes also prohibited slaves from owning any property without the consent of their owners.

Many southern states forbade slaves to sell goods, assuming that anything they had to offer was stolen. A slave could not testify against a white person in court, could not meet with groups of other slaves, and could not travel without the permission of his or her master. The possession of firearms was nearly always forbidden, and in areas where arson was a problem, slaves were not even allowed to light cooking fires without white supervision.

Slaves were not only barred from activities legal for whites, they were also punished more severely than whites for the same crimes. Authorities rarely imprisoned them: slavery itself, with its forced labor and restrictions on travel, was little different from a life sentence, and a slave's absence from the work force would punish his or her master as well. Instead, convicted slaves were whipped or subjected to ear cropping. The death penalty (usually imposed by hanging) was applied to a great many more crimes if the offender were a slave. For example, assaulting, poisoning, or shooting a person with intent to kill was a capital crime, meaning one punishable by death, in much of the South only if the aggressor were a slave and the victim white. The same was true for such crimes as arson, theft, and rape.

To enforce their slave codes southern states organized patrols, which were extensions of the regular state militias. Counties were divided into "beats," in which all free white male residents were required to serve on patrols for one to six months. The codes empowered "patrollers"—as slaves called patrol members—to arrest slaves found off their owners' plantations, to search slave quarters for weapons, and

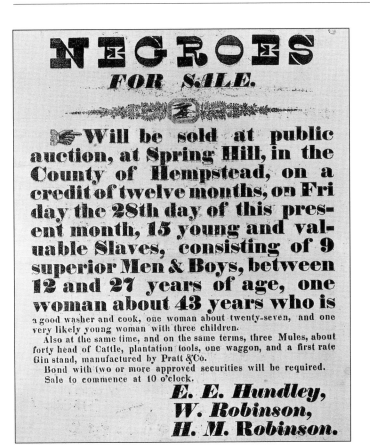

NEGROES FOR SALE.

☞ Will be sold at public auction, at Spring Hill, in the County of Hempstead, on a credit of twelve months, on Friday the 28th day of this present month, 15 young and valuable Slaves, consisting of 9 superior Men & Boys, between 12 and 27 years of age, one woman about 43 years who is a good washer and cook, one woman about twenty-seven, and one very likely young woman with three children.

Also at the same time, and on the same terms, three Mules, about forty head of Cattle, plantation tools, one waggon, and a first rate Gin stand, manufactured by Pratt &Co.

Bond with two or more approved securities will be required. Sale to commence at 10 o'clock.

E. E. Hundley,
W. Robinson,
H. M. Robinson.

A broadside advertising a slave auction. Slaves were legally considered property and could be bought, sold, or seized as payment on debts; slave auctions often included the sale of livestock, furniture, tools, and other property, as shown here.

to break up assemblies of slaves. In many states patrollers were also permitted to punish wayward slaves—and as they were usually unsupervised, often they sadistically abused any black unfortunate enough to cross their paths.

Slaves had virtually no protection from patrollers, vigilante mobs, or their owners. On paper, many states protected slaves from beatings, killings, or summary justice (punishment without trial), but protective laws were often quite weak (a number of states simply fined abusive owners $20) and usually went unenforced in any case. The same was true for laws requiring owners to feed and clothe their slaves properly and laws regulating the type and quantity of work an owner could demand of his slaves. In contrast,

Slaves were rarely imprisoned, since their absence from the work force would affect their owners as well. Instead, wayward slaves were usually beaten or whipped, often publicly, for even slight offenses.

state authorities vigorously enforced laws requiring slaves to obey orders and to submit to punishment.

Though such a system invited abuse, not all slaves suffered equally. Some owners—usually free blacks or members of abolition societies who had purchased slaves in hopes of freeing them—gave slaves free rein. Since many states made it difficult for owners to free their slaves legally, blacks who were owned by free family members or by abolitionists were usually what historian John Hope Franklin termed "virtually free," legally slaves but treated by their supposed masters as complete equals.

Indeed, in 1827 a North Carolinian society of abolitionist Quakers was legally forbidden to purchase slaves because, according to a state supreme court decision that year, "[w]hen Quakers hold slaves, nothing but the name is wanting to render it at once a complete emancipation." Even if a slave's owner treated him as a person, however, he was still considered property by the state and was required to abide by the slave codes. As a result, a slave could be seized and resold should his owner go into debt or die without freeing the slave.

Most southern states prohibited the education of slaves, but sympathetic owners and literate blacks sometimes taught slaves to read and write. A slave's education was often limited to learning a particular job skill, such as blacksmithing, tailoring, or carpentry. Many skilled slaves lived in urban areas. But they were a necessity on large plantations, which were often far from cities and towns where free craftspeople could be hired. Usually "surplus" slaves—those whose labor was not needed by their owners—were taught job skills so that their owners could "hire out" their labor. Hiring out was the common practice of renting a slave to another person for money; a skilled slave would bring a higher price.

Although widespread, the practice of hiring out was controversial—and even illegal in some states. Hired slaves competed directly with white workers, much to the dismay and resentment of the latter. Some owners allowed their slaves to hire out their own time, to bargain on a price much as a free person would. To encourage slaves to seek the highest price for their labor, these owners often allowed them to keep a share of the money they earned. Many southerners sharply criticized this practice because they believed it gave slaves too much independence and enabled them to purchase their freedom.

Slave or free, few people of any race reached the literary level attained by poet and moralist Jupiter Hammon. In 1787 Hammon published his sixth and last work, *An Address to the Negroes in the State of New-York*, the transcript of a lecture he had given in 1784. Historians know little about Hammon beyond these facts: born into slavery on October 3, 1711, he belonged to the Lloyd family of Long Island, New York. The Lloyds seem to have had no objection to educating their slave; they apparently lent him books from their library, and when he was 22 years old, they sold him a Bible. Hammon was probably a preacher among the slaves in Long Island and in Connecticut, where the Lloyds moved during the revolutionary war; he published a number of sermons, and—like most poets of his time—he wrote on strictly religious themes.

Hammon's first work, "An Evening Thought: Salvation by Christ, with Penitential Cries," was the first American poem published by a black author. It appeared in 1760 and was followed in 1788 by "An Address to Miss Phillis Wheatley, Ethiopian Poetess, in Boston," a poetic tribute to the African-American poet. (*Ethiopian* was often used during this period to describe any African American and did not indicate a specific country of origin. Wheatley, kidnapped from her West African home in 1754, was slave to a Boston family, who helped her publish "An Elegiac Poem on the Death of the celebrated Divine, and eminent Servant of Jesus Christ, the late Reverend, and pious George Whitefield" in 1771.)

Hammon's 1779 work, *An Essay on the Ten Virgins*, has been lost, but his first published sermon, *A Winter Piece: Being a Serious Exhortation, with a Call to the Unconverted: And a Short Contemplation on the Death of Jesus Christ* (1782), has survived. In this sermon Hammon refutes an allegation:

> My dear Brethren, as it hath been reported that I had petitioned to the court of Hartford [Connecticut] against freedom [for slaves]. I now solemnly declare that I never have said, nor done any thing, neither directly nor indirectly, to promote or to prevent freedom; but my answer hath always been I am a stranger here and I do not care to be concerned or to meddle with public affairs.

Hammon's disdain for "public affairs" is reflected in his last two works, *An Evening's Improvement: Shewing, the Necessity of Beholding the Lamb of God*

(1783) and *An Address to the Negroes in the State of New-York*. In both pieces, secular political concerns are decidedly second to Christianity and salvation. Hammon states in his *Address*, "Getting our liberty in this world is nothing to our having the liberty of the children of God. . . . What is forty, fifty, or sixty years, when compared to eternity?" But Hammon did not shrink from condemning slavery, even though he felt that it was a slave's duty to trust his fate to God. His *Address* maintains that

> liberty is a great thing we may know from our own feelings, and we may likewise judge so from the conduct of the white people in this war [the American Revolution]. How much money has been spent, and how many lives have been lost to defend their liberty! I must say that I have hoped that God would open their eyes, when they were so much engaged for liberty, to think of the state of the poor blacks, and to pity us. He has done it in some measure, and has raised us up many friends; for which we have reason to be thankful, and to hope in his mercy. What may be done further, he only knows.

Although Hammon died a slave in 1800, he lived to see the passage of manumission legislation in the state of New York and the writing of his owner's will, which directed that a number of the Lloyds' slaves be freed.

Owners like the Lloyds were rare, however, and were destined to become even more uncommon as cotton cultivation expanded in the United States. The vast majority of slaves were engaged in agricultural labor, and most worked on large plantations, growing tobacco, sugar, rice, indigo, and of course cotton. Since only the wealthiest whites could afford large plantations with many slaves, and since these few whites also owned the majority of slaves in the United States, most slaves had relatively little contact with whites. This situation reached its extreme

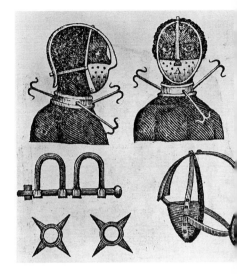

An 1807 illustration of an iron mask, collar, leg shackles, and spurs designed to hinder or prevent a slave's escape.

in the early 1800s in the coastal rice and cotton plantations of South Carolina, where few whites dared
live year-round because of the virulent malaria infest-
ing the area (the disease took a substantial toll on the
slave population). Interaction with whites was so
uncommon that most slaves in the area did not know
English and instead spoke a mix of English and various African languages called the Gullah dialect.

Generally, field slaves worked in groups super-
vised by the owner, a hired overseer, or a slave designated as a "driver." Hired overseers were more likely
than owners to abuse slaves, since they lost no money
if a slave died; drivers were often harsh to impress
their owner and to obtain special treatment for themselves. But owners were by no means exempt from
blame, since they expected overseers and drivers to
get the most possible labor out of the slaves by working them long and hard. Owners, overseers, and drivers routinely beat slaves who worked too slowly,
tried to rest, or performed inadequately. It was not
unusual for a slave on a sugar plantation to labor 18
or 20 hours a day during harvest season, and owners
expected all slaves to work, including small children,
pregnant women, and the elderly.

Weekly food rations for slaves included cornmeal,
lard, meat, molasses, peas, greens, and flour. When
slaves were not in the fields they cooked their own
meals, but during the workday food was prepared by
elderly slaves who could no longer perform heavy
labor. Owners expected slaves to supplement their
weekly rations by hunting, fishing, or raising crops or
livestock on small plots of land set aside for that pur-
pose. These harsh conditions sometimes led slaves to
steal food from their owners; archaeologists have
recently excavated slave cabins with secret root cel-
lars apparently designed to conceal pilfered goods.

Clothing, another necessity, was also scarce.
Some slaves (especially those who worked in the "big

house," as the owner's residence was called) wore their owners' cast-off clothing, but on larger plantations slave women wove coarse cloth to make apparel for all the workers. Some slave women were given fabric to make clothes for their families; others wore cheap, coarse clothing purchased ready-made by their owners. A slave commonly received one set of clothing each summer and one each winter—with or without shoes. A generous owner might give a male slave two pairs of pants, two shirts, and a coat, and a female slave two or three dresses yearly. Children sometimes received only a shirt for the year, and sometimes nothing at all.

Farming slaves lived in cabins near the fields, often in view of the big house. Each family had its own dwelling, usually a small, drafty, sparsely furnished hut with a dirt floor and no windows. These cabins were generally made of stone or wood, but on at least two South Carolina plantations slave huts were made in a traditional African style, with mud walls and thatched roofs.

Conditions were somewhat better for slaves working in the owner's house. Their labor—cooking, cleaning, attending guests, and caring for adults and

Ration day on a southern plantation. Slaves usually received scant weekly food provisions such as cornmeal, lard, and flour, and were expected to supplement their rations by hunting, fishing, and farming in the few hours when they were not working.

Most plantation slaves lived in one-room cabins near the fields they farmed or in view of their owner's house. Small, drafty, and with dirt floors, each cabin housed an entire family.

children—was less physically demanding than field work, and their owners were more familiar with them. Owners who knew their slaves personally were more likely to treat them humanely; a house slave was likely to receive better food and clothing than his or her field counterparts.

House slaves generally viewed their positions as a mark of status, but proximity to owners presented its own problems. A sadistic or controlling owner could make life miserable for a house slave, and females were especially vulnerable to sexual abuse. Nonetheless, conditions were such that house slaves nearly always tried to ensure that their children worked with them in the big house, sometimes resulting in a servant staff several times larger than was needed.

Keeping a family together was a challenge for slaves, who always faced the risk of being sold. The

risk increased after cotton production surged: specu-
lators roamed Maryland and Virginia, looking for surplus slaves to purchase and resell in the new cotton
plantations of the southwest. Although sellers occa-
sionally tried to keep families intact, relatives were
often parceled out to different buyers. The number of
slaves relocated in this manner averaged more than
200,000 during each decade between 1820 and the
Civil War.

A slave marriage was not legally recognized and
could be ended easily by sale. Owners were more
likely to sell men than women because male laborers
generally brought higher prices, but children born to
a female slave became the property of that slave's
owner, so females were potentially valuable com-
modities. Although laws prohibited the separation
by sale of very young children from their mothers,
older children were fair game. Indeed, to increase
their wealth, slaveholders encouraged their slaves to
have children. Sometimes the pressure was subtle: an
owner would encourage a slave to marry by perhaps
offering to purchase a desired mate if he or she was
owned by another. At times an owner exerted more
direct pressure, by urging marriage and by offering
gifts and money to new mothers. In 1792, for example, a Virginia planter promised a woman her freedom if she bore five children; by 1803 she had delivered six, and the planter kept the five oldest children
and freed her and her youngest child. When hints
and promises were ineffective, owners sometimes
resorted to threats; some women were literally forced
to take a husband.

For a slave owner, another advantage of encour-
aging slaves to bear children was that a woman with
a family was much less likely to attempt escape.
"Running off" to seek freedom was in effect a means
of slave resistance. Many successfully attained freedom in the northern United States or Canada; some

A watercolor illustration of a slave wedding dance. Although slave marriages were not legally recognized, they were encouraged by slaveholders as a means to prevent trouble or escape.

hid in the swamps and forests of the South, raiding plantations for food and terrorizing slave owners; some simply stayed near their owner's plantation for as long as possible, resting and slowing down the field or house work.

A more drastic—and desperate—means of avoiding work or sale was self-mutilation, or the cutting off or maiming of one's own body parts, such as fingers or toes. Tragically, suicide was fairly common among slaves, especially those newly arrived from Africa, who tended to be terrified by their captivity. The horrors of slavery were such that, despite rewards for childbearing, slave mothers sometimes killed their babies to keep them from growing up into slavery.

But not all forms of resistance were self-destructive. Slaves often stole, feigned illness to slow work, or engaged in acts of sabotage by breaking farm tools. They burned houses and barns, often targeting the homes of patrollers out on rounds. And despite the threat of almost-certain death, a few attempted to kill their owners, usually with knives, clubs, or poison.

Perhaps as early as 1786 and almost definitely before 1808, a secret organization of militant abolitionists arose to aid slaves in their quest for freedom. Runaway slaves would be smuggled from one safe house to another on their way to the North, following a course that became known as the Underground Railroad. By the 1820s Congress was examining the issue of escaped slaves in Canada, but the existence of the Railroad remained only a rumor for decades. The Railroad's "conductors" were hard at work, however: between 1810 and 1850, as many as 100,000 slaves rode the "train" north to freedom.

Many of the conductors on the Underground Railroad were, not surprisingly, African Americans who had already obtained their freedom. Remembering the plight of their enslaved brethren, free blacks organized and agitated in an effort to extend the "blessings of liberty" to all African Americans. But in a society in which most blacks were slaves, free blacks occupied an often tenuous position.

4

THE MEANING OF "FREE"

Although by the early 19th century most American blacks were enslaved, some had been born into liberty or had been emancipated. Census data from 1790 shows that 59,000 free blacks lived in the United States (approximately 27,000 in the North and 32,000 in the South); by 1830 the number had grown to 319,000. Much of this growth occurred between 1790 and 1810, when several northern states abolished slavery and when few states legally restricted owners from freeing slaves.

During this period the line between slavery and freedom could be disturbingly thin: in many states a free black convicted of certain crimes could be legally sold into slavery. In Virginia, creditors could seize freed slaves and sell them into slavery if their former owner had debts contracted before the slaves' liberation. Most northern states outlawed the kidnapping

In 1792 Benjamin Banneker, a free black Marylander, was hired by President George Washington's surveyor to assist in measuring a site for the young nation's future capital. An astronomer and author of almanacs, Banneker once wrote to Thomas Jefferson, a slave owner, imploring him to cease "in detaining by fraud and violence so numerous a part of my brethren under groaning captivity and cruel oppression."

and reenslaving of free blacks, but such laws were rare in the South.

Under federal and local laws, white Americans had many specific rights and relatively few restrictions, while free blacks had few rights and many limits on their behavior. Even in areas where legal codes were not in themselves racist, white behavior could be as oppressive as law. Slave owners, worried that free blacks would inspire, organize, and lead slave rebellions, often prohibited free blacks from meeting with slaves. Laws of most southern states either forbade free blacks to carry firearms or required them to obtain a gun license. In 1806, Tennessee made it illegal for free blacks to travel outside their county of residence.

Special laws provided harsh punishments for a free black who verbally or physically assaulted a white person. According to an 1806 law in Louisiana, "Free people of color ought never to insult or strike white people, nor presume to conceive themselves equal to the white, but on the contrary that they ought to yield to them in every occasion, and never speak or answer to them, but with respect." Nowhere in America could free blacks testify in court against whites, and they were punished more harshly than whites for the same crimes. U.S. prison statistics for 1826 reflect the lack of legal protection: in Massachusetts, for example, blacks represented 1 in every 73 residents but 1 in every 6 inmates; in New York, whites outnumbered blacks 35 to 1 in the general population, but only 3 to 1 in the prison population; and in Pennsylvania, where 1 in every 34 residents was black, 1 in every 3 prisoners was black. African-American citizens had the right to vote in only a handful of states, and in those states the right was not unconditional. Connecticut, for example, which extended voting privileges to free blacks in 1802, withdrew them in 1814, and New York required that blacks own at least $250 in property

before they were permitted to vote (whites were under no such restriction). Where free blacks could vote legally, hostile local whites often threatened, harassed, and intimidated them into staying home.

All the slave states and many free states prohibited the immigration of free blacks. In 1806, as their numbers increased in Virginia, the state passed a law requiring freed slaves to leave the state within a year or be sold back into slavery. Over the next 15 years or so, other southern states passed similar laws. Even Massachusetts, a relatively progressive state, expelled 240 free African Americans from Boston on the grounds that they were not state citizens.

Those states that did allow the entry of free blacks often required them to document their freedom, present letters attesting to their good character, or deposit a sum of money to be forfeited should they be arrested for any reason. In 1804 Ohio required free blacks to post a $500 bond—a prohibitive sum at

The kidnapping of a free black woman and her child, 1822. By this time several northern states had abolished slavery, but free blacks were under constant threat of being kidnapped and reenslaved.

Richard Allen was cofounder of the Free African Society, the first African-American organization in the country. The Philadelphia-based society was rooted in religious principles and later grew into the African Methodist Episcopal church, one of the largest black religious denominations in the United States.

the time—to guarantee their good behavior. This law was implemented in 1829 when a large number of blacks tried to settle in Cincinnati. The influx prompted racist whites to demand enforcement of the 1804 statute; the city responded by ordering the blacks to post bond or leave the state within 30 days. Cincinnati's black leaders won an extension of the deadline and began searching for a settlement in Canada, but locals were not placated. White mobs roamed black neighborhoods—housing in Cincinnati, as in most cities of the time, was strictly segregated by color—spreading destruction and terror. When a delegation of Cincinnati blacks returned from Canada with the government's invitation to settle and a guarantee of full citizenship rights, more than 1,100 blacks left the city. By the end of 1829 the editor of the *Cincinnati Gazette*, who earlier had supported the eviction, was lamenting the city's loss of its "sober, honest, industrious, and useful" black citizens.

Although black codes often prevented slaves from gathering for religious (or other) purposes, free blacks were encouraged to embrace Christianity, an institution that whites believed was essential to maintaining the social order. Members of many Christian sects—both northern and southern—joined the free blacks in opposition to slavery. (That spirit of common cause would later change drastically, as increasing sectionalism split many denominations into antislavery northern branches and proslavery southern branches.)

White churches may have welcomed free blacks in their congregations, but often black worshipers were segregated from white churchgoers, forced to sit in the back pews or in the balcony. Richard Allen, in his 1833 book, *The Life Experiences and Gospel Labors of the Rt. Rev. Richard Allen*, recounts one such instance in a Philadelphia church in 1787:

A number of us usually attended Church in Fourth Street: and when the colored people began to get numerous in attending the church, they moved us from the seats we usually sat on, and . . . told us to go to the gallery seats over the ones we formerly occupied below, not knowing any better. We took those seats. . . . Just as we got to the seats, the elder [a church official] said, "Let us pray." We had not been long on our knees before I heard considerable scuffling and low talking. I raised my head up and saw one of the trustees . . . having hold of the Rev. Absalom Jones, pulling him off of his knees, and saying, "You must get up—you must not kneel here." Mr. Jones said, "Wait until prayer is over." [The trustee] said, "No, you must get up now, or I will call for aid and force you away." Mr. Jones said, "Wait until prayer is over, and I will get up and trouble you no more." With that he beckoned to one of the other trustees . . . to come to his assistance.

After the prayer, reported Allen, the black congregants "went out of the church in a body, and they were no more plagued with us in the church."

Both Allen and Absalom Jones were men of extensive religious training. Born a slave in Philadelphia in 1760, Allen became a Methodist at 17 and persuaded his owner to allow Methodist meetings on his estate. One such meeting featured a guest preacher who was firmly opposed to slavery. Deeply moved by his sermon, Allen's owner offered him and one of his brothers the opportunity to purchase their freedom. Allen went into business for himself, chopping wood and making bricks during the day and preaching at night, as he traveled through the mid-Atlantic states.

In 1786 Allen returned to Philadelphia, where he met Absalom Jones, a former slave who at 38 had also bought his freedom. Jones had begun his religious education at an earlier age than had Allen; one of his first purchases as a child had been a copy of the New Testament. He had been a prominent and long-standing member of St. George's Methodist Episcopal

Church when Allen was appointed its minister upon his return to Philadelphia.

Both men felt the need for what Allen called "an African church," a place of worship for Philadelphia's black community. The city's white Methodist clergy furiously opposed the idea and barred separate meetings of black Methodists. Allen and Jones decided to create a black organization outside the church, and in the spring of 1787 they established the first black social support organization, the Free African Society. After Jones was pulled to his feet during prayer six months later, he, Allen, and the rest of the black congregants of St. George's left their church and began planning an independent African church in Philadelphia.

The Free African Society, determined to affiliate their new house of worship with the Episcopal church, offered the ministry to Allen. Overwhelmingly loyal to his Methodism, Allen declined the offer. The society then approached Jones, who put aside his doctrinal preference and in the summer of 1794 dedicated the St. Thomas African Episcopal Church of Philadelphia. (Ten years later, the rector of St. Thomas would become the first ordained black Episcopal priest in the United States.)

That same summer Allen established the Bethel Church, a black Methodist institution. Despite the potential for competition between the ministers of Bethel and St. Thomas, Allen and Jones remained friends until the latter's death in 1818, on many occasions joining forces to defend the rights and reputation of blacks in Philadelphia and in the rest of the world. Allen's church thrived—by 1815 Philadelphia's black Methodists outnumbered its white Methodists—and other black Methodist churches sprang up across the country.

White Methodist leaders, far from enthusiastic about the black congregations appearing in their

In 1794 Absalom Jones dedicated the St. Thomas African Episcopal Church of Philadelphia, one of the earliest African-American churches in the country.

midst, constantly harassed Allen and his colleagues. In April 1816 African Americans responded to this treatment by establishing the first fully independent black church in the United States, the African Methodist Episcopal (AME) church. Allen, who was appointed the first AME bishop, continued to lead both the new church and the country's fledgling civil rights movement until his death in 1831. His efforts led essayist David Walker to praise him enthusiastically in his 1829 *Appeal*:

> Richard Allen! O my God! The bare recollection of the labours of this man, and his ministers among his deplorably wretched brethren, (rendered so by the whites) to bring them to a knowledge of the God in Heaven, fills my soul with all those very high emotions which would take the pen of an Addison [the celebrated late-17th-century English essayist Joseph Addison] to portray. . . . Suffice it for me to say, that [his name will] stand on the pages of history among the greatest divines [clergymen] who have lived since the apostolic age, and among the Africans, Bishop Allen's will be entirely preeminent.

Allen also established a day school for black students in 1795 and a society to promote the education of black children in 1804.

Before the 1830s few laws openly restricted the careers available to free blacks, but lack of educational and training facilities kept most African Americans out of higher-paying professional fields. To combat this problem, black leaders founded independent adults' and children's schools, some funded by state governments. By the late 1820s, however, black publications reported growing dissatisfaction with the lack of money and low expectations of black-only institutions—handicaps that were to plague segregated schools for more than a century. Some educational integration did occur: in 1826 Edward Jones and John Russwurm graduated from predominantly white Amherst College and Bowdoin College, respectively, making them among the first African Americans to earn college degrees.

Free blacks began organizing in many other fields as well. The first black theater company, the African Theater, was founded in New York City in 1821 and flourished for several years. The African Lodge of the Fraternal Order of the Free and Accepted Masons was founded in Boston in 1775 by former slave Prince Hall. Hall and other lodge members sent petitions to the Massachusetts legislature protesting the exclusion of blacks from public schools, the kidnapping and selling into slavery of free blacks, and the participation of Massachusetts merchants and sailors in the slave trade. The petition, which was published in the *American Mercury*, led to the enactment of a 1788 law banning the importation, transportation, purchase, or selling of Africans by Massachusetts residents or citizens.

African-American Masons also established lodges in Providence, Rhode Island, and in Philadelphia, where Allen was a member and Jones the lodge mas-

A replica of a wooden clock made by Benjamin Banneker, one of the 18th century's most notable astronomer-mathematicians. The 22-year-old Banneker constructed his clock without instructions or models.

ter. The lodges communicated frequently, and in 1800 Hall, inspired by Allen and Jones, opened the first black school in Boston.

Despite the shortage of formal education, some blacks managed to attain remarkable levels of learning and success. One of 18th-century America's best-known astronomer-mathematicians was Benjamin Banneker, a self-educated black man born free in 1731. The son of a farmer and himself a farmer, Banneker was taught to read by his grandmother but received little formal education. Quiet and bookish, he impressed his neighbors when, at the age of 22, he built a clock that struck the hours. He had no special

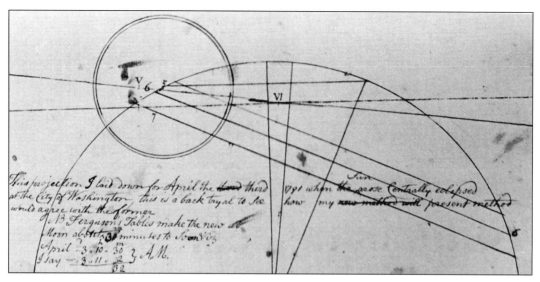

Banneker's diagram of an eclipse on April 3, 1791. Astronomical calculations were an important part of Banneker's almanacs, which also featured political commentary and arguments against slavery and racism.

tools, no books or teacher to instruct him, and no model. He worked from his recollections of the complicated workings of a pocket watch he had once seen. Banneker's homemade wooden clock worked perfectly—and continued to toll for another half century.

When the Ellicotts, a highly educated white family, moved to the area 20 years after Banneker had constructed his clock, they found themselves much impressed by their neighbor's extraordinary intelligence. The teenaged George Ellicott grew especially close to Banneker, to whom he introduced the science of astronomy. Fascinated by the movements of the planets, the farmer borrowed equipment from George and soon demonstrated his formidable mathematical skills by projecting the date of the next solar eclipse. Having discovered what he thought was a minor error in Banneker's calculations, George was further impressed when his neighbor demonstrated that the error was the result of inaccurate information contained in George's own books.

Banneker's obvious talent inspired him to compile an almanac. Annual publications containing astronomical information, meteorological predictions, and witty sayings or poetry, almanacs were very popular in 18th-century America. In 1791 Banneker completed his calculations and sent the finished almanac to a printer, but the printer never published the work, perhaps because of Banneker's race.

But Banneker's efforts were not in vain. The printer had sent the manuscript to George Ellicott's brother Andrew, who had been appointed during the winter of 1791 by President George Washington to survey an area near Maryland designated for the nation's capital (later known as the District of Columbia). Andrew asked George to serve as his assistant, but George suggested Banneker, now 60, instead. Already impressed by Banneker's work, Andrew readily agreed. Throughout the winter and spring of 1792 Banneker kept progress notes, made calculations, and operated the astronomical instruments used in the project.

In March 1792 the *Georgetown Weekly Ledger* reported that Andrew Ellicott was "attended [in his surveying] by Benjamin Banneker, an Ethiopian, whose abilities, as a surveyor, and an astronomer, clearly prove that Mr. Jefferson's concluding that race of men were void of mental endowments [in his *Notes on the State of Virginia*], was without foundation."

Later that year Banneker published the first of six almanacs—the first, he noted in a letter to Andrew Ellicott, "that ever was made in America by a person of my Complection [skin color]." Distributed by abolition societies in Pennsylvania and Maryland, Banneker's almanacs omitted the usual trivia and humor and instead provided political commentary and arguments against slavery and racism. The almanacs also promoted racial pride and an awareness of black history: one issue notes that needles were "first made in London, by a Negro from Spain," and another includes a poem written by former slave Phillis

Wheatley (c. 1754–1784). "That Africans and their Descendants," noted Banneker in introducing the poem, "are capable of attaining a Degree of Eminence in the Liberal Sciences BENJAMIN is not the only proof."

Although Banneker's almanacs were quite popular at the time—they went through 28 editions—he is perhaps best remembered for a remarkable letter he addressed to Thomas Jefferson, then secretary of state, in 1791. On the surface, the letter is merely a polite offer to send Jefferson a complimentary copy of Banneker's soon-to-be-published almanac. Aware, however, that Jefferson was not only the author of the Declaration of Independence but an owner of slaves, Banneker also wrote:

> Sir, how pitiable is it to reflect, that altho [when you wrote the Declaration of Independence] you were so fully convinced of the benevolence of the Father of mankind, and of his equal and impartial distribution of those rights and privileges which he had conferred upon them, that you should at the Same time counteract his mercies, in detaining by fraud and violence so numerous a part of my brethren under groaning captivity and cruel oppression, that you should at the same time be found guilty of that most criminal act, which you professedly detested in others, with respect to yourselves.
>
> Sir, I suppose that your knowledge of the situation of my brethren is too extensive to need a recital here; neither shall I presume to prescribe methods by which they may be relieved, otherwise than by recommending to you, and all others, to wean yourselves from those narrow prejudices which you have imbibed with respect to them, and as Job proposed to his friends "Put your Souls in their Souls' stead," thus shall your hearts be enlarged with kindness and benevolence towards them, and thus shall you need neither the direction of myself or others in what manner to proceed herein.

Jefferson never asked for Banneker's "direction," but he did forward the writer's calculations to the prestigious Academy of Sciences in Paris. "I considered it as a document to which your whole colour had a right for their justification," he said in a letter to Banneker, "against the doubts which have been entertained of them."

Banneker printed his correspondence with Jefferson as an introduction to the 1793 edition of his almanac. He continued to produce almanacs until ill health forced him to discontinue them in 1797. He died nine years later. During the burial of his body, his house burned down, destroying what had been perhaps his favorite possession: the wooden clock he had made a half century earlier.

The accomplishments of such extraordinary trailblazers as Allen, Hall, and Banneker were celebrated among black and abolitionist communities but were known to relatively few others. The turn of the century was instead marked by a series of earth-shattering events that occurred on a French island colony only a few hundred miles south of the United States. When the smoke cleared, the world beheld the first independent black nation in the New World.

5

HAITI

The Haitian revolution originated in Saint-Domingue, a French colony on the large Caribbean island of Hispaniola. (The island also contained the Spanish colony of Santo Domingo, now the Dominican Republic.) Slavery had flourished on Saint-Domingue, site of a vast and thriving sugar industry. By the 1790s the island's slave population outnumbered by six to one all other groups, including a sizable free black population. To prevent revolts, French slaveholders—notably cruel and abusive even among slave masters—had enacted the infamous Code Noir, a set of "black laws" that stood alone in its severity.

The carefully regulated order of Haitian slavery began to break down in 1789 with the onset of the French Revolution, a violent rebellion in France against the French crown that would result in the execution of King Louis XVI in 1793. After the rev-

---

In 1791 the slave population of Saint-Domingue, led by François-Dominique Toussaint-Louverture (here pictured reading a constitution), revolted and took over the northern part of the French colony. The French were unable to regain control, and in 1804, the former slaves established an independent nation, which they named Haiti.

olution, French political power lay in the hands of a group of elected representatives known as the National Assembly. Some, known as Republicans, favored a further weakening of the monarchy and the establishment of a democratic republic. Others, the Royalists, wanted a return to monarchy and refused to recognize the authority of the National Assembly.

Republicans and Royalists vied for power both in France and in its colonies, and in Saint-Domingue the predominantly Royalist slave owners formed militias of armed slaves to help defend their interests, a strategy that would backfire as the situation in Saint-Domingue worsened. In March of 1790 a free mulatto (a person of mixed white and black ancestry), Vincent Ogé, met with a French-based Republican civil rights organization, the Amis des Noirs (Friends of Blacks). Ogé persuaded the Amis to present a petition to the French National Assembly urging that free black colonials be given the same rights as free white colonials. Faced with fierce opposition from white planters, the assembly decided to compromise and passed a vaguely worded resolution giving the vote to free residents, denying it to slaves, and mentioning race not at all.

Ogé knew that Saint-Domingue's whites would never willingly share with blacks the right to vote. Consequently, he obtained implements of persuasion—arms secretly bought from abolitionists in the United States. When colonial authorities refused to enforce the voting resolution, he mobilized a revolt. Ogé and his forces, however, proved no match for the better-armed, more numerous Royalists. Although the rebels achieved several victories, in the end the slaveholders won. They captured and executed Ogé, making him a martyr and an enduring symbol of the unquenchable human thirst for freedom.

Sporadic violence rocked Saint-Domingue over the next year. Although the French National

Assembly passed increasingly liberal laws concerning the rights of blacks, authorities in the Royalist-dominated colony proved increasingly unwilling to enforce those laws. Finally, on the night of August 14, 1791, slave leaders from plantations in northern Saint-Domingue met to plan an uprising. According to witnesses, the meeting finished with a voodoo (or religious) ceremony in which the conspirators pledged themselves to their cause. "Listen to the voice of liberty," they chanted, "which speaks in the hearts of all." A week later slaves rebelled on more than 1,000 plantations, and northern Saint-Domingue exploded in revolution. The rebels besieged the city of Le Cap, where the newly elected

Slaveholders in the French colony of Saint-Domingue were notoriously brutal, even among slave masters. In this scene, slaves are forced to restrain and flog one of their own.

Though a sizable free black population existed on the Caribbean island of Hispaniola by the 1790s, free blacks did not have the rights accorded to whites. When colonial authorities refused to enforce the French government's resolution giving them the right to vote, Vincent Ogé, a free mulatto, mobilized an armed revolt against Saint-Domingue's slaveholders.

colonial assembly had gathered to meet. The violence spread quickly as free black militias took over parts of the southern and western sections of the colony, and smaller but equally bloody outbreaks blazed all over the island.

The French National Assembly, temporarily under the control of an extremely liberal Republican political faction known as the Jacobins, sent military forces to Saint-Domingue. Their objective was to restore order and to stave off the British and Spanish, who saw in the tumult an opportunity to take control of the colony. Since commanders sent to lead the French military forces were Jacobins and members of the Amis des Noirs, they sympathized more with the rebellious blacks than with the Royalist white plantation owners, many of whom eventually fled the colony. But although the French commanders restored peace and even allied themselves with some of the rebels, the Spanish made considerable headway into Saint-Domingue. In 1793 they offered support and military commissions to rebel leaders. Among them was François-Dominique Toussaint-Louverture, a 50-year-old former slave who had risen to prominence among the rebels. Toussaint accepted a commission from the Spanish but rapidly grew exasperated with Spain's continuing support of slavery.

In May 1794 Toussaint and his 4,000 seasoned fighters abandoned the Spanish for the French Republicans. Their change in allegiance was no doubt motivated by the National Assembly's declaration, issued four months earlier, that all slaves in all French colonies were thenceforth free. Toussaint's forces, combined with those of the French Republicans, quickly compelled a Spanish retreat from Saint-Domingue. The armies then turned on the British, whom they expelled from the island in 1798.

By this time very few whites remained in the colony. Most of the French planters had fled, and

French Republicans remained only with the permission of Toussaint, who had, thanks to his almost legendary reputation and military ability, emerged as Saint-Domingue's leader. The proslavery forces, however, were far from defeated. Toussaint never explicitly declared Saint-Domingue independent from France, but he demonstrated considerable autonomy in governing the colony. In 1800, for example, he led a force into neighboring Santo Domingo, where he liberated the Spanish colony's 15,000 slaves.

Toussaint's control of Saint-Domingue did not sit well with France's new ruler. Napoléon Bonaparte, a former Jacobin who had assumed power in 1799, was far more conservative than his former revolutionary allies, especially in regard to slavery. In 1801 he sent a military expedition to the French Caribbean colony of Guadeloupe; its mission—to restore slavery on the island—was successful.

Although Toussaint attempted to fortify Saint-Domingue against invasion, he was hampered by disagreements among his followers and, even more significantly, by his lack of a navy. In 1802, when 16,000 French soldiers landed on Saint-Domingue, Toussaint tried in vain to negotiate a settlement. The French arrested him and transported him to France, where he died after a year of constant mistreatment.

In Saint-Domingue the report of Toussaint's arrest was followed by more bad news: Napoléon had restored slavery and the slave trade to all French colonies. Now the residents of Saint-Domingue understood their ruler's intentions. By October 1802 black military leaders who were previously willing to negotiate with the French led a concerted assault against the French troops on the island. The soldiers responded by slaughtering every black Haitian they could lay hands on. But the French, weakened by months of yellow fever, were no match for the desperate, freedom-seeking blacks. Within a month they retreated entirely. Jean-Jacques Dessalines, a former slave and aide to Toussaint who had assumed power after his leader's arrest, made a rousing declaration as the French departed the battered and blood-soaked island:

> The Independence of St. Domingue is proclaimed. Restored to our primitive dignity, we have asserted our rights; we swear never to yield them to any power on earth. The frightful veil of prejudice is torn to pieces. Be it so for ever! Woe be to them who would dare to put together its bloody tatters!

Reflecting its altered status, the former colony took a new name: on New Year's Day 1804, Saint-Domingue became the independent republic of Haiti.

Many of Saint-Domingue's white former plantation owners had taken refuge in the American South, where their tales of violent slave uprisings were heard with terror. Slaveholders shuddered at the success of the Haitian revolution, and with good reason, for it would inspire similar revolts in America.

In early 1800, Gabriel Prosser, a charismatic 24-year-old slave from Henrico County, Virginia, and his two brothers, his wife, and his best friend began planning an armed uprising against their masters. By early summer the rebels had recruited other slaves to join their revolt, which they hoped to stage on the evening of August 30. They would begin by killing Gabriel's owner, Thomas H. Prosser, then march the six miles from Prosser's farm to the state capital of Richmond, where they would seize the state arsenal and slaughter all the whites they encountered except for Methodists, Quakers (who opposed slavery), and French people. Obviously influenced by events in Saint-Domingue, Gabriel Prosser hoped that he would inspire slave rebellion across Virginia and that

the rebels would gain the support of the French.

On the appointed night, at least 1,000 enslaved black men gathered at a rendezvous point. All seemed in readiness, but Gabriel's plot was doomed. Only hours before the attack was to begin, two slaves, probably hoping for a reward, betrayed the rebels to white authorities. Virginia governor James Monroe, who would later become U.S. president, promptly mobilized troops to guard Richmond and to watch all roads leading to the city from Prosser's plantation. Then, Monroe later wrote, came "one of the most extraordinary falls of rain ever known in our country." The muddy roads to Richmond were flooded. No rebels marched that night.

The next day Monroe ordered local slave owners to "apprehend and commit to prison without delay all the slaves in the county whose guilt [you have] good

Blacks battle French soldiers on Saint-Domingue during the rebellion that led to the founding of Haiti. Inspired by events on the island, Gabriel Prosser in 1800 and Denmark Vesey in 1822 organized armed slave uprisings in the United States.

cause to suspect." Upon interrogating the prisoners, officials learned to their horror that the rebellion, as Monroe described it, had "embraced most of the slaves in this city and neighborhood, and that the combination [conspiracy] extended to several of the adjacent counties . . . and there was good cause to believe that the knowledge of such a project pervaded other parts, if not the whole State."

Despite the reward offered for Gabriel's arrest, he managed to evade capture for almost a month. His pursuers finally cornered him in Norfolk, where he had fled from Richmond aboard the ship of a sympathetic white abolitionist. Tried and found guilty, Gabriel, along with 34 convicted conspirators, was hanged. During the trial, one of the accused men—perhaps Gabriel; the records are unclear—had delivered an impassioned speech:

> I have nothing more to offer than what General Washington would have had to offer, had he been taken by the British and put to trial by them. I have adventured my life in endeavouring to obtain the liberty of my countrymen, and am a willing sacrifice to their cause; and I beg, as a favour, that I may be immediately led to execution. I know that you have pre-determined to shed my blood, why then all this mockery of a trial?

Gabriel's inspiration, Haiti, soon came to embody the fears of violent insurrection haunting slaveholders everywhere. Southern politicians successfully lobbied to prevent the United States from recognizing the new country, and as late as 1826 the mere suggestion that the United States attend a convention of former Spanish colonies to which Haitians had been invited touched off a fiery debate in Congress.

The fear instilled in the American South over events in Haiti was to lead to a major victory for the abolition movement—a federal ban on the importation of slaves into the United States. By 1798 most states had closed off their overseas slave trade; the

revolution in Saint-Domingue inspired the rest to follow suit. In 1803, however, South Carolina not only reopened the trade but imported the first of nearly 40,000 slaves it would absorb over the next four years. In 1807 the first federal anti-importation bill was passed almost unanimously by Congress and signed into law by President Thomas Jefferson. The law set a $20,000 fine for slave importers and demanded the confiscation and sale of their ships and cargo.

The end of slave importation was a turning point in the struggle against slavery. The conditions on board ships carrying slaves from Africa to the New World were horrific, and death rates were high. In addition, fewer slave imports meant higher prices for slaves, which in turn meant that owners were motivated to keep their slaves alive and relatively healthy, rested, well fed, and well housed.

In 1801, Toussaint-Louverture gained control of Santo Domingo, the Spanish portion of Hispaniola. Napoléon, wishing to regain possession of the island, sent General Victor-Emmanuel Leclerc to persuade Toussaint to swear loyalty to France. Toussaint refused to give in but was betrayed by his general, Maurepas, shown here surrendering to Leclerc. Toussaint was forced to surrender and later seized by trickery and deported to France, where he died in 1802 under inhumane conditions.

Some supporters of the anti-importation law were guided by humanitarian concerns, but others backed the law because they knew that most slaves imported into the United States came from the Caribbean, perilously close to Haiti, and that such slaves might have been involved in the struggle for freedom that had rocked the area. Slave owners also feared that unlimited slave importation would result in what they considered racial imbalance, with enslaved blacks vastly outnumbering free whites in large sections of the country. And that, of course, had been precisely the situation in Saint-Domingue on the eve of its first great slave uprising. Ironically, many of the law's supporters were fiercely opposed to the manumission of slaves and did not view the ban as a criticism of slavery or as a first step toward abolition.

Fear of slave uprisings in the United States was not quelled by the passage of the anti-importation law. On the contrary, the Haitian revolts had spurred the passage of even harsher legal restrictions on the activities of blacks, both free and enslaved. In addition, Napoléon's failure to take Saint-Domingue had crushed his hopes of building a New World empire; in 1803 he sold to the United States the enormous Louisiana Territory—830,000 square miles extending from the Mississippi River to the Rocky Mountains and north to the border of Canada. Slavery had long existed in the territory, but by midcentury it would spread to vast proportions, giving the region a chilling reputation as a sure and early grave for slaves.

But for at least one slave, the Louisiana Territory proved a land of opportunity. President Jefferson had quickly organized an exploring expedition for the largely unmapped territory, headed by two experienced frontiersmen, Meriwether Lewis and William Clark. In their party was York, a trusted slave of Clark. A large and extremely powerful man, York proved an excellent outdoorsman and an invaluable member of the expedition. His skill, strength, and endurance led to his inclusion in many of the reconnaissance teams sent out from the main party to explore and map the area and to secure food.

York also proved his worth during the expedition's encounters with the area's Native Americans, whose cooperation and guidance were essential to the mission's success. Despite the language barrier, his outgoing nature and exotic appearance (he was often the first black person the Indians had ever seen) made him a favorite of many tribes.

While he was staying with the Arikara Indians of what is now western South Dakota, York discovered that many of them doubted that he was really human. Capitalizing on the situation, the imaginative explorer told the Arikaras through an interpreter that he had been born wild and had lived off the flesh of children until Clark had captured and tamed him. This unlikely story fascinated the tribe's children, who would flock around the towering black man and flee in delighted terror when he turned toward them, roaring in mock ferocity. At the end of the expedition, Clark emancipated York, who, according to legend, returned to the western interior and became a tribal chief.

York's role in exploring the United States is one example of the many ways in which black Americans—prejudice and slavery notwithstanding—were deeply connected to the fate of their nation. But because many whites were uncomfortable with the idea of a multiracial America, the early 19th century saw the emergence of a movement to "whiten" the country by shipping blacks back to their "homeland," Africa.

6

COLONIZATION AND ITS DISCONTENTS

The colonization movement, a wide-ranging effort to settle blacks in African colonies, began in England in the early 1800s. The movement quickly spread to the slaveholding Americas, and though it drew impassioned supporters and equally ardent opponents in the 1810s and 1820s, it never found unqualified support among any U.S. group. African Americans disagreed vigorously over the merits of various colonization plans and the motivations of those who proposed them; slave owners were no less divided. The intense controversy, combined with the cost of sending people to Africa, kept the movement from succeeding; despite oceans of ink spilled both in defending and in attacking colonization, fewer than 15,000 free American blacks migrated to Africa.

The colonization movement was rooted in a 1772 British legal decision declaring that no one, white or

In 1819 the American Colonization Society was granted a charter to settle a group of free blacks south of Sierra Leone in a colony known as Liberia. The first settlers arrived in 1822, and in 1838 they united to form the Commonwealth of Liberia. In 1847 Liberia, whose flag is shown here, became Africa's first independent republic.

black, who set foot on the British Isles (England, Wales, Scotland, and Ireland) would be considered a slave. Not surprisingly, the decision was followed by a sudden influx of blacks into Great Britain; any American slave who could cross the Atlantic Ocean could claim his or her freedom. Many of these immigrants were poor and possessed neither the education nor the contacts to find work and become self-supporting.

Disturbed by this situation, Henry Smeathman, an amateur botanist who had lived for many years in West Africa, moved to establish a West African colony where, he hoped, the lives of immigrant blacks would be somewhat easier. Smeathman died before his plan reached fruition, but his efforts were continued by Granville Sharp, a social reformer and black-rights supporter. Sharp and his colleagues bought about 20 square miles of land from a local African ruler, and a ship carrying nearly 350 blacks and about 100 whites (many of them wives of the black immigrants) landed on the shore of a small African country, Sierra Leone, on May 9, 1787. Life in the new colony, which the settlers named the Province of Freedom, was far from idyllic, however: disease and attacks by natives devastated the colony, and by 1791 only 64 settlers remained.

The following year the British abolitionist Thomas Clarkson led 1,131 blacks and 100 whites to the Province of Freedom to reinforce the colony, but they too were beset by disease. The French besieged the colony in 1794, and as more blacks arrived from the Americas, disagreements and violence flared among colonists. In 1807 the Sierra Leone Company, a private organization in charge of the colony, turned it over to the British government, which had outlawed the slave trade and ordered the Royal Navy to stop slave ships. When the navy impounded such ships, it set free their captive "cargoes," often in the

A 19th-century view of Freetown, Sierra Leone, where thousands of African slaves were released after the British navy began intercepting slave ships in 1807.

Sierra Leone colony, which grew from 2,000 people in 1807 to 5,000 in 1811.

In 1811, Paul Cuffe, a black American merchant, visited the colony. Cuffe (pronounced CUFF-ee, from the West African word *kofi*, meaning "born on Friday"), the founder and owner of a successful New England shipping company, had become increasingly discontented with the limited prospects for blacks in the United States, and had begun searching for a place where American blacks could "rise to be a people." Cuffe's father, Cuffe Slocum, was a West African who had been sold into slavery at age 10; doubtless he told his son stories about happier times in his homeland.

Cuffe had decided that the only way to end the slave trade was to stop it at its source, in Africa. He believed that slavery's hold on Africa could be broken by introducing the native population to Christianity and to Western education, and he could think of no better missionaries for this effort than America's free blacks. Cuffe hoped that he and other business-oriented blacks could eventually establish African industries that would enrich the continent and provide other means of income for former slave traders.

Cuffe's interest in colonization prompted a former governor of Sierra Leone to invite him to visit the colony. Departing the United States in December

Paul Cuffe, a black American merchant, believed that the slave trade must be abolished at its source—in Africa—and hoped to establish an independent colony where American blacks could "rise to be a people."

1810 in his newest ship, *Traveller*, Cuffe and his cargo of merchandise reached Africa's west coast three months later. There he learned that he could sell few of his goods because he was not British (like many European nations at the time, Great Britain sought to maximize overseas profits by prohibiting foreigners from trading in its colonies). After Cuffe finally persuaded the governor to lift the prohibition, he discovered that the British merchants who controlled the colony's trade would offer him only ruinously low prices for his goods.

Undaunted, Cuffe contacted the colony's black merchants, who introduced him to local African leaders and helped him sell his cargo. Before leaving the colony in May 1811, Cuffe drew up a petition urging the British government to support black American immigration to Sierra Leone and to allow foreign traders to do business in the colony. The petition was well received by Sierra Leone's black settlers, many of whom joined to form the Friendly Society, a mutual-aid organization designed to promote black business interests. Cuffe also received a letter from the African Institution, a British organization founded to promote the welfare of the Sierra Leone colonists. The institution informed him that the British government would grant him a special license for trade between England and Sierra Leone, and urged him to travel to London and obtain the license.

Cuffe arrived in London in July 1811. He obtained his trading permit and visited prominent abolitionists and government officials. After taking on new cargo, he departed for Sierra Leone in September. Cuffe's ship was blocked upon its arrival by orders of the colony's new governor, Charles Maxwell, who held Cuffe for a few days under the pretense of studying his trading license and then allowed the ship to unload only under the close supervision of authorities.

Relations with Maxwell deteriorated further when Cuffe renewed his ties with the colony's black merchants and with the Friendly Society, which the governor distrusted. Despite conflicts with Maxwell and some of the British businessmen of the colony, Cuffe avoided having his trading privileges revoked and managed to sell his cargo and scout potential sites for agricultural and industrial development. Cuffe sailed for the United States in February 1812, intending to return as soon as possible with colonists and goods.

But when Cuffe reached the United States, he discovered that his country and Great Britain were on the verge of war. Trade with Britain had become illegal, and American customs officials impounded his ship at Newport, Rhode Island. Cuffe promptly traveled to Washington, D.C., where he met with President James Madison and Treasury Secretary Albert Gallatin. The men agreed to release Cuffe's ship, and reports of his meetings were printed in several local papers. As Cuffe traveled north, he discovered that he had become something of a celebrity among blacks. He visited Baltimore, Philadelphia, and New York, meeting with black leaders and asking for volunteers for his next colonizing expedition.

Because the War of 1812 dragged on until 1814, Cuffe was unable to sail for Sierra Leone until December 1815. This time his ship carried more than goods: accompanying him were 38 black Americans eager to find a new life in the African colony. They were coolly received by the new governor, Charles McCarthy, who agreed to give the new settlers farmland but forbade Cuffe to sell most of his goods and taxed the remainder so heavily that Cuffe lost all the money he had invested in the expedition.

Nonetheless, when Cuffe left the colony in April 1816, he had some cause for hope. The Friendly Society was thriving despite continued official disregard, and the colonists he had brought had already improved the area's agriculture. Although Cuffe continued to promote colonization until his death in September 1817, he never saw Africa again. Severe economic conditions forced him to focus on rebuilding his fortune, and he could find no one willing to finance another expedition. Although Cuffe's plan of settling Africa may seem unrealistic today, his vision of a self-reliant, economically self-supporting black community free from oppression still resonates.

Cuffe had been approached shortly before his death by members of a new organization called the American Colonization Society, established to promote the transportation of blacks to Africa. The all-white society, launched in Washington, D.C., in late 1816, was not an abolitionist group, nor did it support measures demanding humane treatment of slaves. Its only goal was to settle free blacks—and free blacks only—in Africa.

The society's founder, the Reverend Robert Finley, believed that the establishment of an African colony would benefit free blacks, but many of the members were slaveholding southerners who merely wished to get rid of potentially troublesome free blacks. Senator Henry Clay of Kentucky, one of many prominent proslavery politicians who had joined the organization, claimed that black colonization would "rid our country of a useless and pernicious, if not dangerous, portion of its population."

In the beginning, a number of prominent and successful African Americans—for example, Cuffe and Prince Hall (who may have been born and raised in Africa)—supported the society. Most American blacks, however, soon turned against it, believing that the society regarded nonenslaved African Americans as "bad examples" for slaves. Furthermore, although free blacks often referred to themselves as Africans, the majority were generations removed

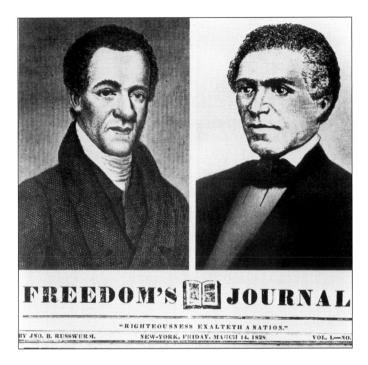

FREEDOM'S JOURNAL

"RIGHTEOUSNESS EXALTETH A NATION."

BY JNO. B. RUSSWURM.   NEW-YORK, FRIDAY, MARCH 14, 1828.   VOL. I.—NO.

Freedom's Journal, *published by Samuel Cornish (left) and John Russwurm (right), was the first newspaper in the United States owned and operated by African Americans. "We wish to plead our own cause," Cornish and Russwurm declared in the first issue. "Too long have others spoken for us. Too long has the publick been deceived by misrepresentations. . . . The civil rights of a people being of the greatest value, it shall ever be our duty to vindicate our brethren, when oppressed, and to lay the case before the publick."*

from Africa and viewed the United States as their home. Many agreed with Richard Allen, who wrote in an 1827 letter to *Freedom's Journal*, "This land [the United States] which we have watered with our tears and our blood, is now our mother country, and we are well satisfied to stay where wisdom abounds and the gospel is free."

Even more disturbing to blacks was the prospect that the American Colonization Society—which included among its members not only Senator Clay but former president Thomas Jefferson, President James Madison, the general and future U.S. president Andrew Jackson, and Congressman Daniel Webster—might acquire immense political strength. The society, they reasoned, might gain enough influence to convince lawmakers to force free blacks to be shipped to Africa. Less than a month after the American Colonization Society was organized, more than 3,000 people crowded into Philadelphia's Bethel

Church to protest colonization. They issued a statement saying,

> We never will separate ourselves voluntarily from the
> slave population in this country; they are our brethren
> by the ties of consanguinity [common ancestry], of suf-
> fering, and of wrongs; and we feel that there is more
> virtue in suffering privations with them, than fancied
> advantages for a season.

Despite the opposition, the American Colonization Society was granted a large sum of money by the
U.S. Congress in 1819 and settled a group of black
colonists south of Sierra Leone in 1822. Known as
Liberia, the colony boasted more than 1,400 black
American residents by 1830. Some were slaves who
had been emancipated on the condition that they
emigrate; others were free southern blacks who had
despaired of succeeding in America's racist society.

One Liberian settler from the relatively progressive Northeast, John Russwurm, had been among the
first black Americans to earn a college degree and
was editor of America's first black abolitionist paper,
Freedom's Journal. His decision to join the colonization movement sparked violent protests, making him
perhaps the first black man burned in effigy by a mob
of free blacks.

John Brown Russwurm, Jr., was the acknowledged
son of a white Jamaican plantation owner and an
unknown black woman, possibly a slave. Born in
1799, Russwurm enjoyed a privileged childhood, living on his father's Jamaica estate until 1807, when he
was sent to Quebec, Canada, to attend boarding
school. At 14, Russwurm moved into his father's new
home in present-day Maine. He attended the local
college-preparatory school, Hebron Academy, taught
in Boston for four years following graduation, and in
1824 enrolled in Maine's Bowdoin College.

During his two years at Bowdoin (because of his

A view of Monrovia, Liberia, several decades after the colony's first settlers arrived.

age and level of education, he was accepted into the college as a junior), Russwurm became acquainted with a number of abolitionist faculty members, some active in the Underground Railroad, others in the American Colonization Society. When Russwurm graduated from college in 1826, he moved to New York City to work as an abolitionist.

A series of editorial attacks on the nation's free blacks, published by several white-owned newspapers, inspired the youthful activist to become involved in the establishment of a black newspaper. Though relatively young and inexperienced, Russwurm was named coeditor along with the considerably older Samuel Cornish, a minister and longtime black activist. The first issue of *Freedom's Journal*, published on March 16, 1827, contained an editorial explaining its reason for being:

> We wish to plead our own cause. Too long have others spoken for us. Too long has the publick been deceived by misrepresentations, in things which concern us dearly, though in the estimation of some mere trifles; for though there are many in society who exercise towards us benevolent feelings; still (with sorrow we

confess it) there are others who make it their business to enlarge upon the least trifle, which tends to the discredit of any person of colour; and pronounce anathemas [curses] and denounce our whole body for the misconduct of this guilty one.

We are aware that there are many instances of vice among us, but we avow that it is because no one has taught its subjects to be virtuous; many instances of poverty, because no sufficient efforts accommodated to minds contracted by slavery, and deprived of early education have been made, to teach them how to husband their hard earnings, and to secure to themselves comfort.

Among the issues debated in the columns of *Freedom's Journal* was the colonization movement, and although both Russwurm and Cornish opposed it, Russwurm's criticism tended to be far more muted. When Cornish left the paper in 1827, readers complained that it suddenly became much less militant.

As sole editor of the paper, Russwurm became increasingly uncomfortable with the growing radicalism of abolitionists, many of whom advocated violence to end slavery. When members of the American Colonization Society approached him in early 1829, they found him surprisingly receptive to their project. *Freedom's Journal* soon reflected Russwurm's shift in viewpoint: editorials critical of colonization no longer appeared in its pages, and Russwurm printed a statement claiming that his earlier views opposing colonization had been "mistaken."

Eventually Russwurm ran an editorial asserting that the race situation in the United States was hopeless. Even if every black lived a thousand years, he stated,

we should be exactly in our present situation: a proscribed [condemned] race, however unjustly—a degraded people, deprived of all the rights of freemen and in the eyes of the community, a race who had no lot nor portion with them. We hope none of our readers will from our remarks think that we approve in the least of the present prejudices in the way of the man of colour; far from it, we deplore them as much as any man; but they are not of our creating, and they are not in our power to remove. [Look to Africa], where the Man of Colour freed from the fetters and prejudice and degradation, under which he labours in this land, may walk forth in all the majesty of his creation—a new born creature—a Free Man!

But the readers of *Freedom's Journal* wanted little short of revolution in the United States, and they were infuriated by Russwurm's change of heart. Their indignation, expressed through hate mail and effigy burnings, forced the editor's resignation at the end of March, 1829. By September he was on a ship bound for Liberia.

Sadly, Russwurm discovered that America's racism reached even to Africa. Doubting that black settlers could govern themselves, the leaders of the American Colonization Society had appointed white agents, many incompetent or prejudiced, to handle the colony's affairs. After seven years of struggle with the society, Russwurm disassociated himself from it and moved to a nearby colony founded by a group known as the Maryland Society, which granted its settlers much more independence. The members appointed Russwurm governor of the colony in 1836. He ran it until his death in 1851, four years after the Liberian colony broke ties with the American Colonization Society and declared itself the Free and Independent Republic of Liberia.

While Russwurm and Cuffe were looking to Africa for a solution to slavery, the issue remained unresolved in the United States. The 1810s and 1820s were not only a heyday of the colonization movement. They were also a time of conflict and compromise as the United States expanded its borders.

7

SLAVERY IN EXPANSION

With the purchase of the Louisiana Territory and the gradual settlement of the Northwest Territory, the United States dramatically increased its borders in a matter of decades. But the expansion did not go unchallenged: various European countries claimed parts of the new territories, and many areas were already occupied by Native American tribes.

The limits of slavery had also become a contentious and divisive national issue. Predictably, the addition of new slave territories in the southwest resulted in more slave uprisings. One of the largest but least documented occurred in January 1811, when about 500 slaves rebelled near the city of New Orleans, Louisiana. Not until the governor had sent in at least 650 soldiers—and the rebels had lost 82 men—was the revolt contained.

The Battle of New Orleans, January 8, 1815. Although they served admirably throughout the War of 1812, blacks had been officially prohibited from joining the U.S. Army. When New Orleans came under threat of attack from Great Britain in 1814, General Andrew Jackson reversed the policy and called upon free blacks to defend their city. Soon after, the New York state legislature passed a law providing for the raising of all-black regiments.

In the North, U.S. expansion led to disputes over territory, shipping, and trade with British-ruled Canada. Tensions mounted steadily, and in June 1812 the United States declared war on Great Britain. At first few blacks fought, largely because Congress had in 1790 excluded them from the federal militia (and many individual states also kept blacks out of their armed services). Great Britain, on the other hand, promised freedom to any slave who reached its lines, and a good number of runaways repaid their liberators by fighting for them.

Although the 1797 law establishing the U.S. Navy excluded no one on the basis of race, the secretary of the navy in 1798 officially forbade the enlistment of blacks and Native Americans. Since recruitment was slow, and since many free blacks worked in the shipping business and were thus experienced sailors, the secretary dropped the racial restrictions a few months after his original order. Although he later reversed himself again, naval ship captains continued to recruit black seamen.

Black sailors became a common sight in the War of 1812. Indeed, when Captain Oliver H. Perry wrote a letter to his superior officer in June 1813, complaining that the men sent to serve on his ships were all "blacks, soldiers [as opposed to sailors], and boys," he received a sharp rejoinder. "I have yet to learn that the color of the skin, or the cut and trimmings of the coat, can affect a man's qualifications or usefulness," the officer replied. "I have nearly fifty blacks on board of this ship, and many of them are among my best men."

That September Perry and his naval troops destroyed the British fleet on Lake Erie, an important strategic victory that paved the way for American troops to invade Canada. Of the 400 men under Perry's command, 100 were black. In July 1814 an American fleet on Lake Champlain annihilated a

much larger British force, destroying what was to be the advance guard of an invasion. The gunnery of the American fleet was devastatingly accurate—and many of the gunners were black.

As the war began winding down in 1814, white volunteers became harder to recruit, and black soldiers and sailors were even more essential. Some 2,500 black volunteers erected defenses for Philadelphia when the city was threatened with attack. In October 1814 the New York state legislature reversed its policy of excluding blacks from the state militia and passed a law providing for the raising of two regiments, each of which would include more than 1,000 free blacks. The law also stated that "it shall be lawful for any able-bodied slave, with the written assent of his master or mistress, to enlist into the said corps. . . . The said slave, at the time of receiving his discharge, shall be deemed and adjudged to have been legally manumitted."

This 19th-century map, showing the original 13 states and subsequent acquisitions, only begins to tell the story of the territorial battles and legislative compromises that allowed slavery to spread throughout the country.

Mick-e-no-pah, the first chief of the Seminole Indian tribe. The Seminole tribe was composed of Indians and blacks who had escaped slavery. They lived in the Spanish territory of Florida when the British established a stronghold there during the War of 1812. The United States later invaded Florida, slaughtering over 1,000 Seminoles and blacks in what would become known as the First Seminole War.

Influencing the decision of the New York state legislature were events in New Orleans, which had been under threat of British attack since September. General Andrew Jackson, commander of the troops defending the city, realized that his forces were seriously outnumbered. Addressing "the Free Colored Inhabitants of Louisiana," Jackson issued a proclamation in September 1814. "Through a mistaken policy, you have heretofore been deprived of a participation in the glorious struggle for national rights in which our country is engaged," said the statement. "This no longer shall exist." The army organized and trained two black regiments in the next three months.

On the eve of the Battle of New Orleans (from which the country emerged victorious and Jackson a national hero), Jackson's adjutant general, Edward Livingston, spoke to the black troops: "I expected much from you. . . . But you surpass my hopes," he said. "The President of the United States shall be informed of your conduct on the present occasion; and the voice of the representatives of the American nation shall applaud your valor, as your general now praises your ardor."

Jackson may have been impressed with his black troops, but they were almost disappointed by him. In his September statement Jackson had guaranteed that "every noble-hearted, generous freeman of color, volunteering to serve during the present contest with Great Britain . . . will be paid the same bounty in . . . lands now received by the white soldiers of the United States . . . [namely] one hundred and sixty acres of land." But because Congress had never officially approved Jackson's decision to recruit African Americans, federal officials questioned their obligation to fulfill his commitment. Eventually, after much agitation on behalf of the veterans, the U.S. attorney general decided in 1823 that because black veterans had fought honorably, they deserved the land promised them whether or not Congress approved.

During the war the British had organized military units in Florida, then nominally Spanish territory, and had established a fort on the Apalachicola River. They were warmly welcomed by the Seminole Indians. A Native American tribe that was a conglomeration of many smaller tribes, the Seminoles had settled in Spanish Florida to escape hostilities with the United States. A substantial number of tribe members were of African descent—the descendants of runaway slaves who had found refuge among the Seminoles. For decades the Seminoles had been fighting attempts by U.S. state and federal forces to reclaim this human "property." Taking advantage of the Seminoles' hostility toward the United States, the British furnished them with guns and encouraged enslaved blacks to escape to the British fort in Florida. Once there, they were free either to move to the British West Indian colonies or to join the Seminoles against the Americans.

Wary of setting off another conflict with the United States or of starting a new one with Spain, the British withdrew from Florida after the War of 1812 and turned over their fort to a group of runaway slaves. Southern slave owners were appalled at the idea of former slaves running a heavily gunned fort just south of the border, and they promptly pressured the federal government to destroy the stronghold. On May 16, 1816, Major General Andrew Jackson ordered General Edmund Gaines to demolish the fort "regardless of the ground on which it stands." Armed with artillery shells and aided by two offshore naval gunboats, Gaines's troops attacked and destroyed the fort. Killed in the action were 270 black women and children who had gathered there for protection.

Gaines's attack created deep animosity between the United States and the Seminole-black alliance.

Henry Clay was Speaker of the House of Representatives when Missouri's proposed statehood threatened the political balance between free and slave states. Clay, known as "the Great Compromiser," is generally acknowledged as the author of the Missouri Compromise, by which Missouri was admitted to the Union as a slave state, Maine entered as a free state, and slavery was prohibited in any new states above the southern border of Missouri.

The conflict persisted until 1818, when Jackson decided to end once and for all Seminole-black resistance in Florida. Gathering an army of 4,000 men, he invaded Florida that spring, slaughtering more than 1,000 Seminoles and blacks—by his own reckoning, about half the area's population. Those captured alive were sold into slavery. Prospects for the survivors of what became known as the First Seminole War (the second occurred in 1835) grew even dimmer in 1819, when the Spanish government officially acknowledged that it had lost control of Florida and turned over the territory to the United States.

Until 1819, questions about the rapid growth of slavery had occasioned little public discussion outside abolitionist circles. But in February of that year New York congressman James Tallmadge, Jr., who had been instrumental in abolishing slavery in his home state, presented two amendments to a bill that would admit Missouri to the Union. Slavery had long been permitted in the region, but the Tallmadge Amendments, modeled on the northern states' emancipation laws, were designed to end it: the first amendment barred the importation of slaves into the new state; the second freed slaves born in the state after they reached 25 years of age.

Ending Missouri slavery required the cooperation of congressmen from southern states, which had long been a bastion of slavery. The proslavery faction of Congress was further embattled later that year, when its northern colleagues moved to abolish slavery in Arkansas Territory, the site of present-day Arkansas and Oklahoma. Though Congress narrowly defeated the attempt to abolish slavery in Arkansas, it deadlocked over the Missouri issue, with the House of Representatives passing the Tallmadge Amendments and the Senate defeating them. In 1820 the Senate devised a compromise: Congress would admit Missouri as a slave state, but would at the same time admit Maine as a free state to keep the South from dominating the legislature. As an extra inducement to the northern states, slavery would be abolished in the Louisiana Territory north of the latitude of 36°30', the southern border of the new state of Missouri.

The Missouri Compromise eventually passed Congress, but not without deepening the country's divisions over slavery and reinforcing its North-South division. "Hell is about to enlarge her borders," asserted Quaker editor Elihu Embree in his abolitionist journal, the *Emancipator*. Meanwhile,

South Carolina's politicians argued that Congress had no right to determine the limits of slavery in the first place.

In addition to expanding slavery's frontier, the admission of Missouri strengthened the federal legal codes that denied citizenship rights to free blacks. Missouri's proposed constitution not only sanctioned slavery, but also demanded that the state legislature pass laws "to prevent free negroes and mulattoes from coming to and settling in this state, under any pretext whatsoever." Although many states had laws restricting the immigration of free blacks, the severity of the Missouri clause and the fact that it was before Congress, not the state legislature—in effect, giving federal endorsement to the idea that blacks had no rights as citizens—caused a furious debate. Many found it impossible to reconcile the Missouri clause with the clause of the U.S. Constitution that reads, "the citizens of each state shall be entitled to all privileges and immunities of citizens of the several states."

"Custom has made a distinction between [African Americans] and other men," a New Hampshire senator remarked during congressional debates, "but the Constitution and laws make none." Representative Charles Pinckney of South Carolina, who had been a delegate to the 1787 Constitutional Convention, disagreed. When the "privileges and immunities" clause was written, Pinckney stated, "I perfectly knew that there did not then exist such a thing in the Union as a black or colored citizen, nor could I then have conceived it possible such a thing could ever have existed in it; nor notwithstanding all that is said on the subject, do I now believe one does exist in it."

Finally, another compromise was reached—one that would, as New Hampshire representative William Plumer, Jr., predicted before its passage, "in fact amount to nothing, but serve merely as a salve to tender consciences." In March 1821, Congress voted to admit Missouri as a state on the condition that the disputed clause "shall never be construed to authorize the passage of any law . . . by which any citizen . . . shall be excluded from the enjoyment of any of the privileges and immunities to which such citizen is entitled under the Constitution of the United States." But because Congress never explicitly stated that blacks were in fact citizens (and would not do so until the Fourteenth Amendment to the Constitution was ratified in 1868), the Missouri legislature eventually excluded free blacks from the state.

After the Missouri Compromise, the spread of slavery seemed unstoppable. In 1823, settlers in Illinois—a state carved from the Northwest Territory, where slavery had been supposedly forever banned in 1787—proposed calling a state constitutional convention to legalize slavery. Abolitionists reacted quickly, mobilizing preachers, newspaper editors, and politicians to educate voters about the true nature of slavery. Although the proposal was defeated at the polls, by the 1820s the moderate abolition methods that had been successful in the early 1800s had proved largely ineffective in ending, subduing, or even containing slavery. After the Missouri Compromise, abolitionists of both races began demonstrating a new militancy—and an increasing willingness to resort to violence.

8

RESISTANCE AND REBELLION

The 1821 Missouri Compromise focused the nation's attention on slavery, and in 1822 events in South Carolina made the institution's explosive potential unmistakable. That year, authorities in the state capital of Charleston uncovered an extensive slave conspiracy led by former slave Denmark Vesey. The state executed or exiled many of the conspirators in the Vesey uprising but by no means eliminated the strong likelihood of further slave insurrection.

Little is known of Denmark Vesey's early life except that he was born in 1767 and that by age 14 he was living as a slave on the Caribbean island of St. Thomas. His owner, slave trader Joseph Vesey, had sold him to a San Domingo planter in 1781, but when the teenager was diagnosed with epilepsy, Joseph Vesey took him back and refunded the buyer's money. Because Denmark's illness made him unsalable, Joseph Vesey made him his personal slave. From 1781 to 1783 Denmark accompanied his owner

---

A former slave who had purchased his freedom, Denmark Vesey became lay pastor of the Hampstead African Church in Charleston, South Carolina, where his impassioned opposition to slavery aroused support for his planned slave uprising.

on several slave-trading expeditions, where he undoubtedly witnessed firsthand the brutalities of the slave business.

In 1783 Joseph Vesey's slave trade profits declined, and he decided to move to Charleston and pursue other forms of business. Denmark had become a skilled carpenter, and as Vesey was not in pressing need of his labor, he began hiring him out, allowing the slave to keep a small portion of his earnings. Denmark purchased lottery tickets with the money he earned. When he won the lottery, he purchased his freedom from Joseph Vesey for $600. The former slave remained in Charleston, where he eventually became a lay pastor at the Hampstead African Church, a local branch of the AME church. A vehement opponent of slavery, Denmark devoured abolitionist literature and publicly chastised all blacks, enslaved or free, who treated whites with deference.

In 1821 Denmark Vesey organized a slave uprising, scheduling the revolt for a summer day when many of Charleston's whites would be out of the city to escape the summer heat. The plan involved mobilizing six battle units: two units would simultaneously converge on the city's main guardhouse and arsenal; one would capture a secondary arsenal; another would take over the shop of a large gun and ammunition dealer (one of the dealer's slaves, a conspirator, apparently had a key to the shop); a fifth unit would act as a mounted defense squad (horses would be obtained through slaves working in the city's stables); and the remaining unit would block the roads into Charleston. Using the confiscated arms and ammunition, the blacks planned to slaughter Charleston's whites and to take over the city on July 14, 1822. Like Gabriel Prosser before him, Vesey believed that the uprising would spark a general slave rebellion throughout South Carolina and that the rebels would be able to count on aid from Haiti.

A view of Charleston, South Carolina, as it looked in the early 19th century. Denmark Vesey's vast plan of revolt involved six battle units organized to overwhelm Charleston's white population and take over the city, preventing escape or outside aid.

Vesey's conspiracy involved as many as 9,000 slaves organized into "cells," small groups of plotters who knew neither the identities nor the roles of the other plotters. Thus, should one conspirator be captured or questioned by authorities, he or she could not betray the larger movement.

Vesey also enlisted several lieutenants to help him lead the movement. One was Peter Poyas, a skilled and literate slave who had been hired out and could travel around Charleston without raising suspi-

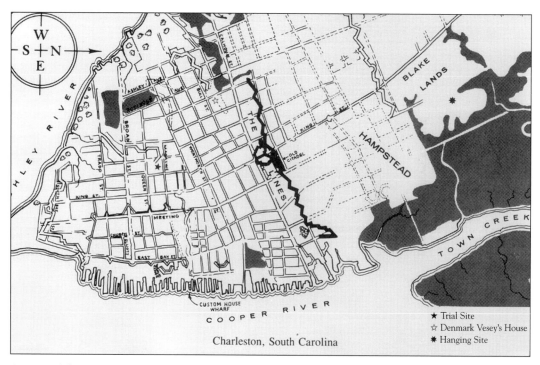

★ Trial Site
☆ Denmark Vesey's House
✳ Hanging Site

Charleston, South Carolina

A map of the city of Charleston, South Carolina, in 1822, showing the trial and hanging sites for Denmark Vesey and his collaborators. Despite precautions, Vesey's conspiracy was revealed to white authorities by a slave, and he was forced to postpone and then cancel his attack. City officials arrested 131 blacks, including Vesey, and he was hanged with five others on July 2, 1822.

cion. Poyas personally recruited 600 conspirators. Rolla and Ned Bennett, two slaves in the home of South Carolina governor Thomas Bennett, informed the movement of the activities of authorities. Painter Jack Glenn collected funds from slaves to purchase weapons and horses, while Monday Gell, a harness maker, recruited slaves from the stables to provide the planned cavalry with mounts. The most flamboyant leader was Gullah Jack, an Angolan-born slave regarded as a powerful sorcerer.

Vesey and his men spent the spring months recruiting slaves, using a number of tactics. According to one conspirator, Vesey "was in the habit of reading to me all the passages in the newspapers that related to St. Domingo [Haiti], and apparently every pamphlet he could lay his hands on, that had any connection with slavery." He told slaves that the majority of Americans opposed slavery, and even claimed that the Missouri Compromise had officially ended slavery but that the local authorities had refused to comply with federal law. He also stressed the possibility of support from Haiti. At one point, Vesey gave a letter to the cook of a Haiti-bound ship, asking that it be delivered to the country's president. He apparently hoped that if Charleston proved impossible to hold, his rebels could flee to Haiti.

But Vesey and his lieutenants realized that some people should not be approached. Poyas told a conspirator to "take care and don't mention [the conspiracy] to those waiting men who receive presents of old coats, etc., from their masters, or they'll betray us." Unfortunately, not all of Vesey's people followed that advice. On May 25, 1822, a conspirator, William Paul, approached house slave Peter Prioleau. According to Prioleau's later statement to the authorities:

> After some trifling conversation [Paul] remarked with considerable earnestness to me. Do you know that something serious is about to take place? to which I replied no. Well, said he, there is, and many of us are determined to right ourselves! I asked him to explain himself—when he remarked, why, we are determined to shake off our bondage, and for this purpose we stand on a good foundation; many have joined, and if you will go with me, I will show you the man who has the list of names who will take yours down.
>
> I was so much astonished and horror struck at this information, that it was a moment or two before I could collect myself sufficient to tell him I would have nothing to do with this business, that I was satisfied with my condition, that I was grateful to my master for his kindness and wished no change. I left him instantly, lest, if this fellow afterwards got into trouble and I had been seen conversing with him in so public a place, I might be suspected and thrown into difficulty.

Prioleau informed the authorities, who arrested Paul on May 30. At first he denied knowledge of the conspiracy, but after a night of interrogation, Paul named Poyas and another slave, Mingo Harth, as

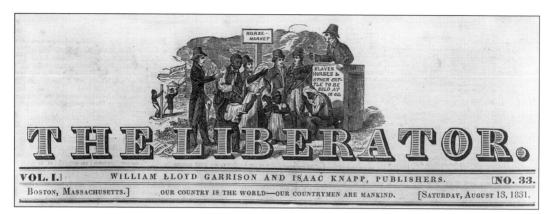

VOL. I.]   WILLIAM LLOYD GARRISON AND ISAAC KNAPP, PUBLISHERS.   [NO. 33.

BOSTON, MASSACHUSETTS.]   OUR COUNTRY IS THE WORLD—OUR COUNTRYMEN ARE MANKIND.   [SATURDAY, AUGUST 13, 1831.

The Liberator, *one of the best-known abolitionist newspapers of the 19th century, was established in 1831 by William Lloyd Garrison, the white founder of the American Anti-Slavery Society. In its first issue, Garrison declared, "I will be as harsh as truth, and as uncompromising as justice. On this subject, I do not wish to think, or speak, or write, with moderation. . . . I am in earnest—I will not equivocate—I will not excuse—I will not retreat a single inch—AND I WILL BE HEARD."*

conspirators. Poyas and Harth were brought before Charleston's mayor and city council the next day. When asked about the planned uprising, the two quick-witted men simply broke into roars of laughter. Investigators found no evidence to incriminate them, so they were released.

Fearful of further leaks, Vesey changed the proposed day of attack to June 16, a month earlier than the original date. But authorities clamped down on the movements of the city's blacks, making communication between the conspirators impossible. The day before the scheduled uprising, Vesey, realizing it would fail, called off the attack and began destroying lists of conspirators and other evidence of his plot. On June 17, however, city officials, who had indeed been cultivating spies and informers, arrested 10 conspirators, including Poyas, Monday Gell, and Ned and Rolla Bennett. By June 23 they had captured 121 more blacks, including Vesey. Five days later, Vesey was tried and convicted. He and five of his coconspirators were hanged outside Charleston on July 2, 1822.

Although authorities would execute 35 others, Vesey's skillful method of organizing prevented them from discovering the identities of all the conspirators—a mystery that terrorized the state's slave owners. No less disturbing was the plot's feasibility. "You cannot think how cunningly devised that scheme was," wrote a Charleston banker in an 1822 letter to an acquaintance. "Had the execution been as well supported, many of us this day would not have been left to tell the tale."

In fear and anger, South Carolina authorities promptly expanded the black codes, assigning white guardians to watch free blacks, banning the practice of hiring out, and forbidding free blacks from Mexico, South America, or the Caribbean to enter the state. Vesey's church was closed, its pastor driven from the city.

But whites soon discovered that increased oppression did not ensure security. On Christmas Eve of 1825, arsonists started a fire in Charleston that destroyed $80,000 in property; it was followed by almost nightly fires for the next six months. Slaves were universally blamed for the fires, and some were attacked by mobs.

Resistance to slavery also took less violent—if no less dedicated—forms. In 1821, white abolitionist Benjamin Lundy founded an antislavery paper, the *Genius of Universal Emancipation*. Eight years later, he hired a fiery 22-year-old, William Lloyd Garrison, as his assistant. Garrison would found the radical abolitionist journal the *Liberator* in 1831 and would become a prominent white abolitionist.

Black abolitionists understood the power of the press as well. One of the earliest—and in many ways, most historically important—full-length abolitionist publications was *The Interesting Narrative of the Life of Olaudah Equiano, or Gustavus Vassa, the African, Written by Himself*, printed in London in 1789 and in New York in 1791. The book, which went through eight printings in five years, is a firsthand account of Equiano's experiences as a free African, as a slave in the New World, and as a freedman and abolitionist in England. Born in Benin (present-day Nigeria) in

An illustration depicting a stereotypical view of slaves as childlike and carefree (this page) stands in stark contrast to the brutal realities of slave life (facing page).

1745 to a local chief, Equiano and his sister were kidnapped by slavers in 1765. After a long journey to Africa's west coast, Equiano was sold to European traders and taken to the New World. His measured yet highly disturbing descriptions of the torturous Atlantic crossing and of the brutalities he witnessed as a slave in Virginia and in the West Indies doubtless opened many eyes to the true nature of slavery.

After years of saving, Equiano purchased his freedom in 1766. But the danger and poor treatment facing free blacks in the New World disgusted him, and he left for England the following year. Shipping out of British ports, he worked as a seaman, adding

Turkey, Italy, Central America, and the Arctic to his already extensive travels. In 1781 Equiano emerged as one of London's leading abolitionists by campaigning to publicize the case of the British slave ship *Zong*. (Luke Collingwood, skipper of the *Zong*, had thrown more than 130 sick African captives overboard to collect insurance on them.)

Although Equiano never returned to Africa, he did assist with the founding of the colony in Sierra Leone, serving as commissary of the African colony's stores. In an unofficial capacity, he publicly revealed that some of the whites involved in founding the colony intended to reenslave blacks once they reached Africa. Equiano's most important contribution to the abolitionist effort, though, was his book, published eight years before his death in 1797. Its clear prose and unsentimental manner present a vivid picture of the horrors of slavery, from the stench of a slave ship's hold to the tortures of the plantation and the tears of families torn apart by sale.

Forty years after the U.S. release of Equiano's memoirs—the first book published by a slave or former slave in a southern state—a poetry collection by slave George Moses Horton, *The Hope of Liberty*,

"Cruelty is the fruit of the system," declares the caption of this picture, which accompanied an article describing a slave mother who killed her children and herself to avoid having the boys sold. The story underscores the overwhelming hopelessness and brutality of a life of slavery.

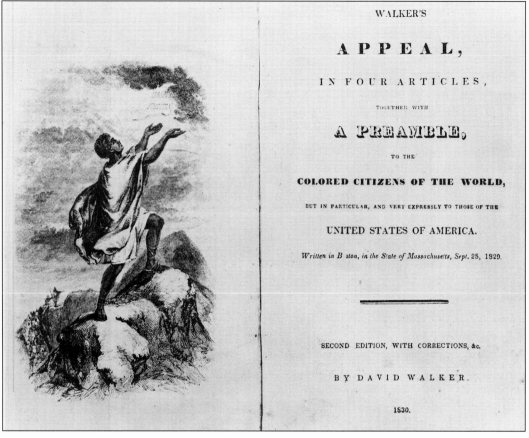

WALKER'S

APPEAL,

IN FOUR ARTICLES,

TOGETHER WITH

A PREAMBLE,

TO THE

COLORED CITIZENS OF THE WORLD,

BUT IN PARTICULAR, AND VERY EXPRESSLY TO THOSE OF THE

UNITED STATES OF AMERICA.

Written in B ston, in the State of Massachusetts, Sept. 28, 1829.

SECOND EDITION, WITH CORRECTIONS, &c.

BY DAVID WALKER.

1830.

David Walker ultimately lost his life in the struggle for black freedom, but his fiery Appeal, *first published in 1829, galvanized into action the abolitionist movement in America and inspired countless others to join the battle for liberty.*

appeared. A Chapel Hill, North Carolina, fruit seller, Horton was discovered by local students, who commissioned him to compose their love poems. But the money Horton earned from selling his poems and fruit was not nearly enough to purchase his freedom; his book was published by a local abolition society whose members hoped to help him raise the necessary sum. Sales were poor, however, and it seemed that Horton would die a slave, a prospect he lamented in his poem "Slave's Complaint":

> Must I dwell in Slavery's night,
> And all pleasure take its flight,
> Far beyond my feeble sight,
> Forever?

Horton continued to write, and in 1837 *The Hope of Liberty* was reissued as *Poems by a Slave*. A new collection, *Poetical Works*, was published in 1845. (A collection entitled *The Museum* may have been printed before *Poetical Works*, but no copies have been found.) Horton's chance for freedom came at the outbreak of the Civil War in 1861, when he fled to a Union army camp in Raleigh. After his emancipation, Horton published *Naked Genius* (1865), his largest collection. He lived in Philadelphia for the remainder of his life.

Perhaps because Horton's editors sometimes softened the tone of his antislavery sentiment, on the whole his poetry stirred little controversy. The same is true of the more militant *Ethiopian Manifesto, Issued in Defence of the Black Man's Rights, in the Scale of Universal Freedom*, published in 1829 by Robert A. Young. But another antislavery work appearing that year provoked fierce debate that not only brought new life and militancy to the abolitionist movement but consumed the life of its writer: *David Walker's Appeal, in Four Articles; Together with a Preamble, to the Coloured Citizens of the World, but in Particular, and Very Expressly, to Those of the United States of America*.

David Walker was born in North Carolina in 1785, the son of a slave father and a free mother. Under the state's legal codes, children inherited the status of their mothers, so Walker was born free but was, by his own account, a close witness to slavery. According to his *Appeal*, Walker traveled the country extensively before settling in the 1820s in Boston, where he opened a small used-clothing shop on the waterfront. In 1827 *Freedom's Journal* was established, and Walker became the paper's Boston agent and a contributor. After John Russwurm sailed for Liberia in 1829, Russwurm's former coeditor, Samuel Cornish, founded a new journal, *The Rights of All*, and Walker helped distribute that paper in Boston as well.

Walker soon began to look for another podium from which to air his views, and in September 1829 he wrote his *Appeal*, which he published at his own expense. The lengthy pamphlet is an impassioned, strongly worded manifesto denouncing slavery, the situation of free blacks, and the conduct of racist whites. In a typical passage, the deeply religious Walker warns slave owners that the days of slavery are numbered:

> I declare, it does appear to me, as though some nations think God is asleep, or that he made the Africans for nothing else but to dig their mines and work their farms, or they cannot believe history, sacred or profane. I ask every man who has a heart, and is blessed with the privilege of believing—Is not God a God of justice to *all* his creatures? Do you say he is? Then if he gives peace and tranquillity to tyrants, and permits [slave-holders] to keep our fathers, our mothers, ourselves and our children in eternal ignorance and wretchedness, to support them and their families, would he be to us a God of *justice*?
>
> I ask, O ye *Christians!!!* who hold us and our children in the most abject [miserable] ignorance and degradation, that ever a people were afflicted with since the world began—I say, if God gives you peace and tranquillity, and suffers [allows] you thus to go on afflicting us, and our children, who have never given you the least provocation—would he be to us a *God of justice?* If you will allow that we are MEN, who feel for each other, does not the blood of our fathers and of us their children, cry aloud to the Lord of Sabaoth against you, for the cruelties and murders with which you have, and do continue to afflict us.

Walker organized his *Appeal* into a preamble and four articles. The first article, entitled "Our Wretchedness in Consequence of Slavery," compares the enslavement of Africans in the United States to that of the biblical Israelites in Egypt, and bitterly concludes:

The condition of the Israelites was better under the Egyptians than ours is under the whites. I call upon the professing Christians, I call upon the philanthropist, I call upon the very tyrant himself, to show me a page of history, either sacred or profane, on which a verse can be found, which maintains, that the Egyptians heaped the *insupportable insult* upon the children of Israel, by telling them that they were not of the *human family*.

Can the whites deny this charge? Have they not, after having reduced us to the deplorable condition of slaves under their feet, held us up as descending originally from the tribes of *Monkeys* or *Orang-Outangs*? O! my God! I appeal to every man of feeling—is not this insupportable? Is it not heaping the most gross insult upon our miseries, because they have got us under their feet and we cannot help ourselves?

The last three articles of the *Appeal*—"Our Wretchedness in Consequence of Ignorance," "Our Wretchedness in Consequence of the Preachers of the Religion of Jesus Christ," and "Our Wretchedness in Consequence of the Colonizing Plan"—vigorously decry the situation of both enslaved and free blacks and attack the inhumanity and hypocrisy of racist whites.

Walker saw no excuse for slavery, and he was certain that the institution would be divinely punished. In his third article he exclaims, "I tell you Americans! that unless you speedily alter your course, *you* and your *Country are gone!!!!!!* For God Almighty will tear up the very face of the earth!!!"

Unlike many preachers and abolitionists, Walker did not expect God to "take us by the hair of our heads and drag us out of abject wretchedness and slavery." Instead, he openly encouraged enslaved blacks to revolt whenever the opportunity arose, and condoned violence and killing:

If you commence, make sure work—do not trifle, for they will not trifle with you—they want us for their slaves, and think nothing of murdering us in order to subject us to that wretched condition—therefore, if there is an *attempt* made by us, kill or be killed. Now, I ask you, had you not rather be killed than to be a slave to a tyrant, who takes the life of your mother, wife, and dear little children? Look upon your mother, wife and children, and answer God Almighty; and believe this, that it is no more harm for you to kill a man, who is trying to kill you, than it is for you to take a drink of water when thirsty; in fact, the man who will stand still and let another murder him, is worse than an infidel, and, if he has common sense, ought not to be pitied.

Not surprisingly, *Walker's Appeal* horrified white slave owners—and many white abolitionists as well. A Boston newspaper, the *Columbian Centinel*, claimed that the pamphlet was "one of the most wicked and inflammatory productions that ever issued from the press." Many southern states reacted to the *Appeal* by imposing severe penalties for circulating abolitionist literature among slaves. Georgia prohibited the employment of black typesetters, and Walker's home state of North Carolina made teaching a slave to read and write a criminal offense.

Nevertheless, the pamphlet circulated widely throughout the country, and it went through three editions in nine months. Through Walker's maritime connections, the pamphlet was easily smuggled into the South. In response, many slave states began restricting the movements of black sailors. By 1830 ominous rumors were circulating in the South: it was whispered that up to $3,000 was being offered for Walker's death and $10,000 for his capture. On June 28, 1830, Walker was found dead near the doorway of his shop—the victim of poison, many abolitionists maintained, although the cause of death was never positively determined.

Walker lost his life in the struggle for freedom, but his *Appeal* and his legacy lived on. The widely circulated news of his death, combined with growing public awareness that half measures could never end slavery, set a new standard for abolitionists. The antislavery movement would become a crusade, a struggle in which people sacrificed their comforts, their livelihoods, and sometimes their lives to end human bondage. Ultimately a devastating war would eliminate slavery in the United States, but only after the African-American fight for freedom had blazed for three centuries.

FURTHER READING

Blackburn, Robin. *The Overthrow of Colonial Slavery, 1776–1848.* New York: Routledge, 1988.

Borzendowski, Janice. *John Russwurm.* New York: Chelsea House, 1989.

Campbell, Edward D. C., Jr., ed. *Before Freedom Came: African-American Life in the Antebellum South.* Charlottesville: University Press of Virginia, 1991.

Conley, Kevin. *Benjamin Banneker.* New York: Chelsea House, 1990.

Diamond, Arthur. *Paul Cuffe.* New York: Chelsea House, 1989.

_____. *Prince Hall.* New York: Chelsea House, 1992.

Franklin, John Hope. *From Slavery to Freedom: A History of Negro Americans.* 5th ed. New York: Knopf, 1980.

Freehling, William W. *Prelude to Civil War: The Nullification Controversy in South Carolina, 1818–1836.* New York: Harper and Row, 1968.

_____. *The Road to Disunion: Secessionists at Bay, 1776–1854.* New York: Oxford University Press, 1990.

Kaplan, Sidney. *The Black Presence in the Era of the American Revolution, 1770–1800.* Greenwich, CT: New York Graphic Society, 1973.

Klots, Steve. *Richard Allen.* New York: Chelsea House, 1991.

Litwack, Leon F. *North of Slavery: The Negro in the Free States, 1790–1860.* Chicago: University of Chicago Press, 1961.

Walker, David. *David Walker's Appeal, in Four Articles; Together with a Preamble, to the Coloured Citizens of the World, but in Particular, and Very Expressly, to Those of the United States of America.* 1829. Reprint. Edited by Charles M. Wiltse. New York: Hill and Wang, 1965.

INDEX

MARY BARR SISSON has an A.B. in English and American Language and Literature from Harvard-Radcliffe University. She currently lives in New York City, where she works as a writer and editor.

CLAYBORNE CARSON, senior consulting editor of the MILESTONES IN BLACK AMERICAN HISTORY series, is a professor of history at Stanford University. His first book, *In Struggle: SNCC and the Black Awakening of the 1960s* (1981), won the Frederick Jackson Turner Prize of the Organization of American Historians. He is the director of the Martin Luther King, Jr., Papers Project, which will publish 12 volumes of King's writings.

DARLENE CLARK HINE, senior consulting editor of the MILESTONES IN BLACK AMERICAN HISTORY series, is the John A. Hannah Professor of American History at Michigan State University. She is the author of numerous books and articles on black women's history, as well as the editor of the two-volume *Black Women in America: An Historical Encyclopedia* (1993). She has also written a collection of essays entitled *Hine Sight: Black Women and the Re-Construction of American History.*

PICTURE CREDITS

Abby Aldrich Rockefeller Folk Art Center, Williamsburg, VA: p. 48; The Bettmann Archive: pp. 2 (frontispiece), 88-89, 91, 92, 94; Bibliotheque Nationale, Paris, France: p. 73; Corbis-Bettmann: p. 71; Corner House Publishers: pp. 16-17; Culver Pictures, Inc.: pp. 79, 85, 101; Delaware Art Museum, Wilmington, Delaware: p. 22; Historical Society of Pennsylvania: p. 57; Kent State University Press, 1983: p. 102; Library of Congress: pp. 19, 53, 104, 106; Painting by Dorothy Wright/Collection of City Hall, Charleston, South Carolina: pp. 98-99; Schomburg Center for Research in Black Culture, New York Public Library: pp. 28-29, 31, 34, 36-37, 39, 40, 43, 45, 46, 50-51, 67, 80, 83, 107, 108; Schomburg Center for Research in Black Culture, New York Public Library, Astor, Tilden & Lenox Foundation: pp. 21, 54, 64-65, 68, 76-77; Silvio Bedini; p. 60; Smithsonian Institution: p. 59.